TIBETAN AMULETS

TIBETAN AMULETS

Tadeusz Skorupski

WITH AN INTRODUCTORY PREFACE BY
Per Kvaerne

Orchid Press

TIBETAN AMULETS
Tadeusz Skorupski

Published by:
ORCHID PRESS
PO Box 1046,
Silom Post Office,
Bangkok 10504, Thailand

www.orchidbooks.com

Copyright © Orchid Press 1983, 2000, 2009.

Protected by copyright under the terms of the International Copyright Union: all rights reserved. No part of this publication may be reproduced in any form or by any means, electronic or mechanical, including photocopying, recording, or by any information storage.

Front cover: Tibetan amulet case (*ga'u*); silver, turquoise and coral. Height 12 cm., width 8.3 cm., depth 3.8 cm. Collection of Susan Weitzman Conway.

Back cover: Folded amulet and wrapping cloth, contained within *g'au* illustrated on front cover. Both photographs copyright and courtesy of Susan Weitzman Conway.

ISBN-10: 974-524-120-2
ISBN-13: 978-974-524-120-6

TABLE OF CONTENTS

Preface vii

Introduction 1

One Hundred and Nine Amulets 11

One Hundred and Two Protective *Cakras* 52

Selected Glossary 121

About the Author 124

PREFACE

Thor's hammer, Fatimah's hand, the sacred scarab—all occupy an ambiguous position on the borderline between magic and religion. The use of charms and amulets is as timeless and universal as man's belief in supernatural beings and forces, invisible but nonetheless real elements of existence. So deeply rooted in the very fabric of human culture is this belief that it almost always survives even when organized religion decays or is destroyed, as the innumerable mascots decorating the front windows of cars all over the world so vividly testify.

Perhaps there are few cultures in which the use of charms, spells and amulets plays a more conspicuous role than in Tibet. This book by Tadeusz Skorupski therefore illuminates a fundamental aspect of Tibetan religion, or rather, the Tibetan view of the world. The author rightly stresses the fact that the use of amulets is an integral part of Buddhism, and by no means a non-Buddhist or pre-Buddhist practice with its 'inferior' origins thinly disguised by Buddhist symbols and *mantras*.

The charms and amulets reproduced here are taken from two short works included in the *Rin-chen gter-mdzod*, the enormous compilation of 'revealed' (the Western sceptic would say 'apocryphal') texts, so-called 'treasures' (*gter*), compiled by Kong-sprul Blo-gros mtha'-yas (1813-1899), one of the greatest scholars of all times in Tibet and a prominent exponent of the East Tibetan 'eclectic' (*ris-med*) movement. Born in a Bonpo family and thoroughly familiar with the Bonpo religion, he was later trained in a Nying-mapa monastery, and was, during most of his adult life, connected with the Kagyutpa school. His religious scholarship thus had an exceptionally broad basis. Following the pioneering work of E. Gene Smith which appeared in

1970,[1] a careful and more detailed biography of Kong-sprul has been published by Dieter Schuh in 1976.[2]

Considering their actual importance in the daily life of the Tibetans, relatively little has been written on the subject of their charms and amulets. Emil Schlagintweit published a number of wood-block amulets in 1863,[3] and further material was made available by L. A. Waddell in The *Gazetteer of Sikhim* in 1894 as well as in *The Buddhism of Tibet or Lamaism*, which appeared the same year.[4] Two more recent works, however, provide a great deal of information: René de Nebesky-Wojkowitz, *Oracles and Demons of Tibet*,[5] and Nik Douglas, *Tibetan Tantric Charms and Amulets*.[6]

Although charms and amulets may be worn on different parts of the body and at different times according to the circumstances, they are usually kept—together with various other consecrated or otherwise magically potent objects and substances—in a box, styled *ga'u*. The use of the *ga'u* seldom failed to be noticed by Western travelers:

> "...every Tibetan woman, however poor, wears on her breast a small box of turquoise set in gold, in which are enclosed spells, charms and prayers written on paper. The men too carry charm-boxes, but of a different type and made of brass or silver, often

---

[1] *Kongtrul's Encyclopaedia of Indo-Tibetan Culture, Parts 1-3*, ed. Lokesh Chandra, Satapitaka Series 80, New Delhi 1970, Introduction by E. Gene Smith, pp. 1-87.

[2] Schuh, Dieter, *Tibetische Handschriften und Block-drucke. Teil 6. (Gesammelte Werke des Kon-sprul Blo-gros mtha'-yas)*, Verzeichnis der orientalischen Handschriften in Deutschland, Band XI, 6, Wiesbaden 1976, pp. xxiii-lxxviii.

[3] Schlagintweit, Emil, *Buddhism in Tibet*, London 1863; reprint London 1968, Plates XI, XIII; attached plates 15-18.

[4] *The Gazetteer of Sikhim*, Calcutta 1894; reprint Bibliotheca Himalayica Series I Vol. 8, New Delhi 1972: L.A. Waddell, "Lamaism in Sikhim", pp. 241-392. See Plates XIII-XIX and pp. 338-353. *The Buddhism of Tibet or Lamaism*, London 1894, Second ed. 1934: reprint London 1959, 1967, and New York 1972, pp. 387-419 (chap. XV "Sacred Symbols and Charms").

[5] Nebesky-Wojkowitz, René de, *Oracles and Demons of Tibet. The Cult and Iconography of the Tibetan Protective Deities*, The Hague 1956; reprint with an introduction by Per Kvaerne, Graz 1975. See in particular pp. 481-537.

[6] Douglas, Nik, *Tibetan Tantric Charms and Amulets. 230 Examples Reproduced from Original Woodblocks*, New York 1978.

with an opening in front to show the small image of a god carried within. The men's charm-boxes are usually hung round the neck, but are sometimes too bulky to be worn, in which case they are carried by a servant. The men also wear amulets and charms sewn up in leather pouches and tied round their arms".[7]

"...the charm-boxes...which are invariable adorned with a lump of coral, are to contain a slip of paper, on which is written the usual formula 'Om Mani-Pe-mi-Hom'. No Tibetan is ever without one of these, no matter how poor or dirty he may be. A miserable yak driver, with perhaps no home, and no worldly possessions but a bit of serge for a coat, will invariably have a charm-box, which may be worth some twenty or thirty taels".[8]

The *ga'u* may also be attached to the hair,[9] and animals, too, may be protected by *ga'u*.[10] Its contents may be of the most diverse kind:
"...round their necks the people carry amulet boxes, without which no Tibetan ventures far. These are packed with a cheap

---

[7] Hayden, Sir Henry, and Cesar Cosson, *Sport and Travel in the Highlands of Tibet*, London 1928, pp. 114-115.

[8] Gill, William, *The River of Golden Sand. The Narrative of a Journey through China and Eastern Tibet to Burmah*, 2 vols, London 1880, vol. II pp. 112-113.

[9] Op. cit. p. 113.

[10] Roerich, George N., *Trails to Inmost Asia. Five Years of Exploration with the Roerich Central Asian Expedition*, New Haven 1931.

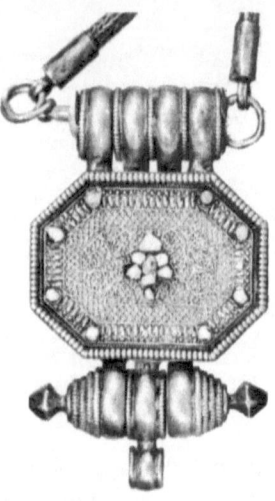 

little image of clay, a few grains of sanctified wheat, two or three written charms and a torn scrap of a sacred katag, orininally thrown over the shoulders or head of some famous image. Pills, too, may be found in the box, red pills certified to contain some speck of the ashes of the *Guru* Rinpoche."[11]

The function of charms may be either protective or destructive, i.e. designed either to protect the bearer or to harm an enemy.

A well-known instance of the tragic consequences of the Tibetans' firm faith in the protective power of charms was the massacre of Tibetan soldiers—by an eyewitness called "the slaughter of helpless men"[12]—during the engagement at Tuna on March 30th 1904 during the British military expedition to Lhasa. The Tibetan soldiers—utterly untrained, impressed peasants—wore amulets which they apparently believed would make them invulnerable to British bullets. Instead, the Tibetans were mowed down by the hundreds. Edmund Candler, the Daily Mail correspondent, himself wounded, witnessed their retreat:

> "As my wounds were being dressed I peered over the mound at the rout. They were walking away! Why, in the name of all their Bodhisats and Munis, did they not run? There was cover

---

[11] Landon, Percival, Lhasa. *An Account of the Country and People of Central Tibet and of the Progress of the Mission Sent There by the English Government in the Year 1903-4*, London (rev. ed.) 1906, p. 209.

[12] Candler, Edmund, *The Unveiling of Lhasa*, London 1905, p. 146.

behind a bend in the hill a few hundred yards distant, and they were exposed to a devastating hail of bullets from the Maxims and rifles, that seemed to mow down every third or fourth man. Yet they walked!

It was the most extraordinary procession I have ever seen. My friends have tried to explain the phenomenon as due to obstinancy or ignorance, or Spartan contempt for life. But I think I have the solution. They were bewildered. The impossible had happened.

Prayers, and charms, and *mantras*, and the holiest of their holy men, had failed them. I believe they were obsessed with that one thought. They walked with bowed heads, as if they had been disillusioned in their gods."[13]

However, charms may also have an aggressive, destructive function—as this book amply illustrates. Ekai Kawaguchi, traveling in Tibet around the turn of the century, describes an attempt made on the thirteenth Dalai Lama's life by the former regent, the abbot of the Tengyeling monastery in Lhasa in 1901:

"Shortly before my arrival in Lhasa this high post was occupied by a distinguished priest named Temo Rinpoche. His steward went under the name of Norpu Che-ring, and this man was charged with the heinous crime of having secretly made an attempt on the life of the Dali Lama by invoking the aid of evil deities... A piece of paper containing the dangerous incantation was secreted in the soles of the beautiful footgear worn by the Dalai Lama, which was then presented to his Holiness. The incantation must have possessed an extraordinary potency, for it was said that the Grand Lama invariably fell ill one way or another whenever he put on these accursed objects. The cause of his illness was at last traced to the foot-gear with its invocation paper by the wise men in attendance on the Grand Lama.

This amazing revelation led to the wholesale arrest of all the persons suspected of being privy to the crime, the venerable Temo Rinpoche among the rest."[14]

---

[13] Op. cit. pp. 144-145.

[14] Kawaguchi, Ekai, *Three Years in Tibet*, Madras 1909; reprint Orchid Press / Bibliotheca Himalayica, Kathmandu 2006, p. 375.

Another instance of similar practices took place in the course of the struggles for power following the death of the thirteenth Dalai Lama in 1933. One of the protagonists of this struggle was Lungsha, a young and ambitious official. Summoned to the Potala by the Cabinet,

"Suddenly fearing that too much was known of his intrigues, Lungsha endeavoured to flee, but was grasped by one of the gigantic monk door-keepers. In the struggle Lungsha's arm was broken and a loaded pistol fell from the pocket of his robe. At the same time one of his boots came off and, from the inside of the boot, two small pieces of paper fell on the floor. Lungsha seized these and, putting them into his mouth, tried to swallow them; but a monk throttled him and recovered one piece on which was written the name of Trimon Shap-pe. Presumably Kapshupa's name was on the other. It appeared that Lungsha had been endeavouring to kill his enemies by witchcraft in the same way that the Regent of Tengye-Ling Monastery had attempted to bring about the death of the young Dalai Lama... Lungsha was put in prison."[15]

Tibetan charms and amulets are not a thing of the past, nor are they any longer the exclusive property of the Tibetans themselves. In May 1973 a number of strange objects were found partly buried in the sand on the beach of the Danish island of Anholt. Among black candles, a tuft of horse hair, and pieces of human bone was found a brass box containing, among other things, a Tibetan woodblock amulet of a common type used as protection against disease. Clearly the lonely beach had been the scene of a black mass, although the participants were never discovered. Probably they were unaware of the exact significance of the Tibetan charm they had used. Yet on a dark and windswept beach in Denmark the image of a Tibetan demon chained hand and foot and bound by powerful *mantras* had perhaps been the object of emotion and faith just as strong as it had been for many centuries on "the Roof of the World".[16]

Per Kvaerne

---

[15] Chapman, F. Spencer, *Lhasa the Holy City*, London 1940, p. 92.

[16] Alver, Bente Gullveig, "Blaesten om Anholt", *Tradisjon. Tidsskrift for folkeminnevitenskap*, 4 (Oslo 1974), pp. 1-20. See ill. no. 11 on p. 16.

Ga'u or Tibetan amulet box. This and the other four illustrated here are reproduced with the kind permission of Ms. Barbara Adams, Kathmandu. Photo: David Keith Barker.

INTRODUCTION

The amulets (*srung-ba*) and the protective *cakras* (*srung-'khor*) are reproduced here from two short works included in *Rin-chen gter-mdzod* which was compiled by *'Jam-mgon blo-gros mtha'-yas*, one of the most prominent thinkers and writers of Tibetan Buddhism in the 19th century. The first work belonging to the *bLa-ma dgongs-'dus* tradition is entitled *Srung-'bum rdo-rje 'phreng-ba*. It was discovered by one of the greatest Nyimapa treasure discoverers (*gter-ston*) *Sangs-rgyas gling-pa* at a place called *Pu-ri phug-mo-che*. The second work discovered in the red *mChod-rten* at Samye (*bSam-yas*) by the treasure discoverer *sNa-nam 'bog-pa thub-rgyal* is entitled *Srung-'khor brgya-rtsa-pa* with a subtitle *gTsug-lag gto-bcos rgya-nag gting-rdzogs-su grags*. Both these works are in volume 42 (*thi*) of the recently republished *Rin-chen gter-mdzod* by *mKhyen-brtse Rin-po-che* who currently lives in Bhutan, and in volume *di* of other Tibetan block-print editions.

The drawings reproduced here were done by my Tibetan friend Ngawang Drodul (*Ngag-dbang 'gro-'dul*) who lives near Marpha in the district of Mustang in Nepal. In interpreting some textual problems I was helped by Ponlob Tendzin Namdak (*dPon-slob bsTan-'dzin rnam-dag*) who is at present the chief teacher at the *Bon-po* monastery at Dolanji in Himachal Pradesh, India.

The Tibetan texts apart from obvious misspellings and a number of difficult passages and obscure terms are rather easy to follow. Most of the *mantras* inscribed on the amulets and the protective *cakras* are written correctly. Several mistakes that were recopied from the original by my scribe were left uncorrected mainly to draw the expert reader's attention to the fact that one does meet quite often with similar or greater mistakes on the consecrated amulets whose efficacy is never questioned. However, in my translations of such *mantras*, I have accounted for the mistakes. A somewhat difficult part of this work was to find English equivalents for the names of various plants, wild animals and diseases; the names of different deities or malignant spirits for obvious reasons had to be left in Tibetan. Whenever I was not certain or could not produce English equivalents I have left the Tibetan names or inserted them in brackets. Furthermore it must be made clear here that the descriptions of the amulets apart from the *mantras* inscribed on them in Tibetan are not literal translations of the Tibetan text. I have considered it quite sufficient for this work to extract and provide the essential information.

My main purpose in reproducing these drawings and providing descriptions is to draw attention to an important aspect of Buddhism, not only of Tibetan Buddhism, which many people nowadays are likely to regard as mere superstition or even as black magic, classing it probably as a form of popular religion beneath the regard of serious religious teachers. However Buddhism in Tibet has been thoroughly pervaded by such magical beliefs and all classes of believers have always subscribed to them, from the lamas who actually provide such amulets, recommending their use, down to the simplest peasant. A recent article by Jampa Panglung draws attention to the Indian tradition concerning the Buddha *Śākyamuni* himself and his sanctioning of a spell against snake-bites in the *Vinaya* (Monastic rules) of the *Mūlasarvāstivādin* School. There is no doubt that such spells, whatever their pre-Buddhist sanctions may be, form part of the general Indian Buddhist tradition as transferred to Tibet.[1] Those who are aware of the vast variety of cultural wealth which came to Tibet as part of the Buddhist teachings, will not be surprised at the mingling of what one might describe as popular and higher religious elements. In the western world such things as amulets, astrology, prognostication and similar preoccupations were looked upon with disfavour by the Christian Church and their practitioners, especially where black magic was suspected, were dealt with vigorously. Buddhism on the other hand has been able to accept such elements without contradicting its fundamental teachings, especially those of the later period, according to which one may make use of any means

---

[1] J.L. Panglung, 'Zwei Beschworungsformeln gegen Schlangenbiss in Mulasarvastivadin-vinaya'. *Heilen und Schenken*, Wiesbaden 1980, pp. 66-71.

helpful in controlling natural forces, in eliminating evil, whether in the form of demons or malevolent humans, and thus to promote one's own and others' good.

The amulets and the protective *cakras* are a very interesting reflection of ordinary life in Tibet. One can see through them how much the Tibetans in their daily lives depend on and are afraid of various local deities and different demoniac powers which can cause damage, bring epidemics and natural catastrophes. The number of amulets designed against a whole range of illnesses and plagues, against bandits and wild animals seem to be a good indication of how much they suffer from them. They are also a good example of how much their ordinary life is motivated and pervaded by religion. The Tibetans turn towards religion for almost anything, be it trading, suffering from severe cold, desiring progeny, destroying enemies and so forth.[2]

Another interesting aspect of Tibetan Buddhism on which the amulets and the protective *cakras* throw light is the classification and the number of the vast variety of different local deities, demons and personified forces of nature.

It is well known that during the propagation of Buddhism in Tibet a firm effort was made to eliminate all the indigenous beliefs and deities which existed in Tibet before the propagation. The Buddhist religion took roots but it has never succeeded in eliminating certain aspects of the pre-Buddhist religion, in particular some powerful local deities. A number of mountain and local deities have been simply incorporated into the Buddhist pantheon and given the role of the protectors of the newly introduced religion. *Padmasambhava* was credited with extraordinary magical powers by means of which he subdued and converted many powerful gods and demons. The gods and demons of lesser importance were simply abandoned. However, the names and at times vague descriptions of different local gods and demons survived in some religious writings and in particular in oral tradition. Very often, apart from their names or a general definition of their sphere of influence, we do not possess any other information. A large number of the amulets and the protective *cakras* reproduced here are devices against such different

---

[2] For description and interpretation of the Tibetan folk religion the reader is referred to Giuseppe Tucci's *The Religions of Tibet*, translated from German, London 1980, chapter 6.

malignant demons and spirits. A clear definition of these demons and spirits cannot be gained from the descriptions of the amulets and the protective *cakras* but their impact on human life and their sphere of activities are relatively well defined.

One Buddhist classification, of gods and demons of lower rank, groups them into eight classes (*lha-srin sde-brgyad*). They are:

1. *Lha* – white in colour
2. *bTsan* – red in colour
3. *bDud* – black in colour
4. *gZa'* – variegated
5. *dMu* – brown
6. *Srin-po* – man-eating demons
7. *rGyal-po* – guardians of temple treasures
8. *Ma-mo* – female demons who cause diseases

When the above list is compared with different names of gods and demons in the amulets and the protective *cakras* it becomes quite evident that not all the gods and demons are included in it. The division into eight classes is rather general and artificial, and the definition of each class is equally general and vague.

Another classification, more detailed and of non-Buddhist origin, which is found in *Deb-dmar* offers a division into nine groups.

1. *gNod-sbyin* – Usually they are considered to be the same as the Indian *yakshas*. However, not all of them are of Indian origin. They are of harmful nature, cause epidemics and diseases and demand bloody sacrifices. A number of them were converted into temple protectors.
2. *bDud* – They are very similar to *dMu* listed below. They live in upper spheres and are manifestations of various aspects of the sky. Their king lives in a black castle of the *bDud*. They can cause harm with regard to places (*gnas*), body (*lus*), and different activities (*las*). They were exorcised by *gShen-rab*, the founder of the reformed *Bon* religion, and instructed to fight against the foes of the *Bon-po* religion.
3. *Srin-po* – These are considered to be the same as the India *rakshasas*.
4. *Klu* – To this group belong different snake-deities living in wells, lakes, rivers and oceans.

5. *bTsan* (and *The*) – This is one of the most powerful classes of demons. With the introduction of Buddhism into Tibet, many of them fell into oblivion, some were included among the *gNod-sbyin* and some converted into the protectors of the Buddhist Law. They are placed in the intermediate space but they seem to be present almost everywhere. They are classed according to the places in which they live; *gnam-btsan* (sky-*btsan*), *gangs-btsan* (glacier-*btsan*), *brag-btsan* (rock-*btsan*) and so forth.

The, originally a separate group, were incorporated among *bTsan*. They were believed to inhabit three regions: the sky (*gnam*), intermediate space (*bar*), and the earth (*sa*). Thus they were called *gnam-the*, *bar-the*, and *sa-the*.

Under the *The* were listed the *The'u-rang* a numberless group of lesser demons who very often acted as retinues of several *dharmapalas* (*chos-skyong*). In a later period *The* and *The'u-rang* were considered to be the same. The *The'u-rang* were believed to live in lower regions of the sky and in the atmosphere. Their leader was called *gNam the 'u dkar-po*. In some texts they are said to have been born from the fat of the golden cosmic tortoise. They are of evil nature, cause quarrels, disunity, bring premature death, harm children and influence the weather.

6. *Lha* – After the introduction of Buddhism they were paired with the Indian *devas*. Before that they were considered to be celestial beings of more benign nature than other classes. They are described as being white in colour in opposition to the *bDud* who are black. In this class are included many gods who do not dwell in the celestial spheres. Thus we find among them such gods as *phrag-lha* - god over one's shoulder, *ma-lha* (mother's god), *pho-lha* and *mo-lha* (male and female gods), *thab-lha* (hearth-god), *srog-lha* (life-god), *lam-lha* (path-god), *tshong-lha* (trade-god), etc.

7. *dMu* – Their abode is in the upper spheres, namely in the sky. In their nature they are similar to the *bDud* but their description and definition remain rather vague. In some writings they are divided into *dMu-chen* (great *dMu*) and *dMu-phran* (minor *dMu*).

8. *'dre* – These are the spirits of malignant character. They spread mortal diseases and bring sudden death. Almost anything harmful

can be called a *'dre*. There is a great number of *'dre* and their activities seem to affect almost every aspect of human life. Very often they are divided into five groups: a) *za-'dre* (food-*'dre*), b) *god-'dre* (*'dre* who cause losses of different kinds), c) *gshed-'dre* (*'dre* of vengeance who bring death), d) *chu-'dre* (*'dre* who live in water), and e) *gson-'dre* (living-*'dre* who bring material losses).

9. *'Don-'dre* – They are listed as a separate class but are difficult to distinguish from the previous group.

Yet another division, independent of Buddhist influence, distinguishes three classes of gods and demons:

1. *gNyan* – Generally they are described as inhabiting the upper space but from their individual names it is quite evident that they also live and act in different places. Thus we have *gnam-gnyan* (sky-*gnyan*), *gangs-gnyan* (glacier-*gnyan*), *mtsho-gnyan* (ocean-*gnyan*), *brag-gnyan* (rock-*gnyan*) and others. They are considered to be harmful and cause different diseases.
2. *Sa-bdag* – They are practically undistinguishable from the *gNyan*. They live in particular places: *sa-bdag* (master of the soil). They are considered to be of indifferent nature but can be good or bad depending on whether they are placated or offended.
3. *Klu* – They are the same as the 4th class of the previous classification.

The above three classifications, although they provide lists of the major groups of gods and demons, they do not include all the names and the descriptions provided, apart from general characteristics, nor do they make a clear distinction between various groups. It is difficult to establish the definite character of each group and to demarcate their differences. What is apparent from the general characteristics is the nature of all the gods and demons of lower rank. They are endowed with mysterious and magic powers by means of which they influence the course of nature and affect human life. Most of them are of malignant disposition and require to be worshipped and placated in order to reduce and prevent their evil influences.[3]

There are other groups of spirits, referred to in the amulets and the protective *cakras*, which are not listed in the above classifications. They are mostly found in the *rNying-ma-pa* and *Bon-po* literature. Among those is the class called *sri*. They are divided into thirteen groups. Their father, called *gNam gyi bya-nag gshog-chags*, and the mother, called *Sa yi byi-gshog*, had thirteen eggs from which were born thirteen different kinds of *sri*. From the first egg that hatched were born the *sri* with human bodies and wolf heads. They lived on mountain tops and devoured male beings. They were called *pho-sri* (male *sri*). From the second egg were born the *sri* who had human bodies and camel heads. They lived in oceans, devoured female beings and were called *mo-sri* (female *sri*). From the third egg were born those with human bodies and weasel heads. They lived under beds, devoured children and were called *chung-sri* (child *sri*), Those from the fourth egg had human bodies and *garuda* heads, lived in the mountains of the *bDud*, consumed the life power of the *Ma-mo* and were called *bDud-sri nag-po* (black demon *sri*). From the fifth egg were born the *bTsan-sri dmar-po* (red *bTsan-sri*). They had human bodies and owl heads, and lived in the mountains of the *bTsan*. From the sixth egg were born those with human bodies and pig heads. The lived in temples and were named *rGyal-sri dkar-po*. Those born from the seventh egg lived in the places where different valleys meet and were called *Dam-sri*. From the next egg were born those with snake heads, who were called *kLu-sri sngon-po* (blue snake *sri*) and lived in waters. Those born with yak heads inhabited the frontiers of the enemy countries. They were called *dGra-sri dar-ma*. Those born from the tenth egg had stag heads, dwelled on the edges of weapons and were called *grisri ngan-pa*. From the eleventh egg were produced the fox-headed *sri*. They lived on the bodies of relatives and harmed old people. The horse *sri* occupied the summits of nine different mountains. They caused harm to people who traveled away from home. From the thirteenth egg were born

---

[3] For more detailed descriptions of different classes of gods and demons see Giuseppe Tucci, *Tibetan Painted Scrolls*, Roma 1949, reprinted in Bangkok 1999, p. 717 ff. For a complete study of the main groups of Tibetan gods and demons see René de Nebesky-Wojkowitz, *Oracles and Demons of Tibet*, The Hague 1956.

the *sri* who had goat heads. They lived in caves bringing misfortune and harm to cattle.[4]

The above description, one of several, does not present an exhaustive list of this class of spirits. There are many other kinds of *sri*. Thus we meet with *gNod-sri* (injury *sri*), *'chi-sri* (death *sri*), *rta-sri* (horse *sri*) and the like. It seems that the *sri* have been related to different classes of more prominent demons as is evident from the above description of their origin and activities (*bDud-sri*, *kLu-sri* etc). One the whole they are divided two general groups of *pho* and *mo sri*—male and female *sri*.

Another group of spirits which seems to be related to *sri* are the *bse* (also written *se* and *bsve*). Like the *sri* they are classed in relation to more powerful demons such as *bDud* and *bTsan*.

bGegs are obstacle-producing demons. In particular they obstruct religious ceremonies. Almost every ritual begins with a short rite for averting the *bGegs*. The classes of *'Gong-po* and *rGyal-po*, which seem to be related to each other, are very little known.

A considerable insight into the understanding of different classes of gods and demons is gained from a *Bon-po* description of the origin of the world in which the cosmos is described as a *ga'u* (=box) with a lower and an upper part, with the creation taking place as an emanation of white and dark light and the male and female principles interacting with each other. Here the dead (*mtshun*) and their active counterparts *te* or *the* are clearly distinguished from the living by not being endowed with life-power (*bla*). There is a clear line drawn between the underworld and the gods. The *Bon* priests specialized in suppressing the demons of the underworld, in exorcising and taming any forces hostile to mankind. The class of the *Srin* (*srin-po* and *srin-mo*) demons of the underworld who influenced greatly the nature and origin of men and the spirits of the dead were looked upon as perpetrators of various difficulties and obstructions to the life and existence of the living. The concept of such obstructive forces (very similar to some Iranian ideas) created in the Tibetan imagination a whole range of personified evil spirits. On the other hand the gods (*lha* and especially *srid-pa'i lha*) of

---

[4] Nebesky-Wojkowitz, op. c., p. 300 ff.

which the early Tibetan kings were manifestations were styled as benign and of good disposition.[5]

A clear picture of various classes cannot be gained either from the Buddhist or the *Bon-po* sources. It is necessary to study both religions in order to understand different classifications and the whole historical development; but that is a long and arduous task.

Finally, the reader's attention is drawn to the fact that the amulets and the protective *cakras* reproduced here belong to one particular tradition. They do not represent the whole spectrum of Tibetan amulets. There is a variety of amulets used by different religious traditions or by different religious orders.[6]

Amongst the Tibetans there are many different ways of designing and making amulets. Some amulets consist of pieces of paper inscribed with magical spells, wrapped in a cloth or wound with threads and carried about the neck or on the body. Others consist of elaborate diagrams and drawings and are inscribed with many spells and *mantras*. One kind of protective device with which one meets quite often are the charm boxes called *ga'u*. Usually they are made of silver and contain magical spells, relics of saint lamas or holy images and other items which are believed to possess magical powers. A *ga'u* when it is small is often carried around the neck. When of a larger size, it is attached at the waist or kept at home.

The efficacy of the amulets is said to be in the power of the *mantras* and spells inscribed on them. However, the more learned lamas stress that the amulets can only bring the desired result when a person has the right inner disposition and firm conviction that they have the magical power to protect.

---

[5] See Erik Haarh, *The Yar-lung Dynasty*, G.E.C. Gad's Forlag, Köbenhavn 1969, pp. 17ff, and 269ff.

[6] For other studies of the Tibetan amulets see: *The Gazetteer of Sikhim*, reprinted in the Bibliotheca Himalayica series, New Delhi 1972, pp. 338-46; René de Nebesky-Wojkowitz, op. c., chapter XXVI; Nik Douglas, *Tibetan Tantric Charms and Amulets*, New York 1978. In the last work are reproduced 230 examples, mainly from wood-blocks, of different kinds of amulets and charms of both Bon-po and Buddhist traditions. The amulets described here are reproduced photographically in Nik Douglas' book on pages 225 and 226. However his reproduction is from another short work of which the title is not given and only a sample of descriptions is provided in English.

ONE HUNDRED & NINE AMULETS

The set of one hundred and nine amulets in based on the Four Rites (*las-bzhi*). The Four Rites are four different ritual activities, the structure of which is fundamentally the same but their purposes differ. The first one is called the pacifying rite (*zhi-ba'i las*) and it is used to pacify demons, obstructive powers and forces of nature, enemies and the like. The second rite is called the enriching rite (*rgyas-ba'i las*) and it is used to bring prosperity and the increase of merit. The subduing rite (*dbang-las*) is used to bring under control demons, obstructive forces and enemies. The fierce rite (*drag-po las*) is employed for destroying demons and enemies. The fifth rite known as the all-purpose rite (*tshogs-las*) comprises all the Four Rites which are performed at the same time during one ritual activity. The amulets listed below, depending on their purposes, relate to one of the above rites. They are made to bring happiness and prosperity, to eliminate evil of various kinds, and to protect those who wear them against harm.

The person who draws and consecrates the amulets should first take refuge in the Three Jewels, generate the Thought of Englightenment and beseech his *guru*, his chosen deity, and the *dakini*. He should draw all the amulets in accordance with the drawings provided and on appropriate materials. All the *mantras* should be in printed letters (*dbu-cen*) and without punctuation marks.

The drawings below represent only the central parts of the amulets. A fully drawn amulet consists of seven concentric areas separated from each other by circumferences (see drawing A). The centre of each amulet inscribed with a mystic letter and the first circumference with an appropriate *mantra*, are different. The *mantras* and the spells on the subsequent circumferences are the same for all the amulets. The complete order of the *mantras*, the

spells, and the sacred syllables is as follows:
1. The centre is inscribed with an appropriate mystic letter. In a number of the *rNying-ma-pa* texts these mystic letters are referred to as the script of the *dakinis*; shortly known as *mkha'yig*. Although some of the mystic letters provided below are easily recognizable as letters of the Tibetan alphabet or their modifications, it is believed that they are secret, incomprehensible to human beings, and endowed with magic powers.
2. The first circumference is inscribed with the *mantra* which invokes the *guru*, the chosen deity and the *dakini* to protect all the attainments (*siddhi*).[1] The *mantra* is followed by an appropriate invocation which defines the purpose of the amulet.
3. On the third circumference one draws eight petals and eight syllables *Hrī* inserted between two punctuation marks (*shad*).
4. The fourth circumference is divided into ten sections each of which is inscribed with the syllable *Hūṃ*.
5. The edges of this circumference are inscribed with the letters of the alphabet and the inside with the *mantra* for the protection of the body, speech, and mind. The appropriate invocation inscribed on the first circumference is also added here.
6. The sixth circumference is inscribed with the salutation to the Buddha, the Doctrine (*dharma*), and the Buddhist Community (*saṅgha*), followed by the *mantras* of five deities, invoking for their protection.
7. On the last circumference are inscribed the *mantra* of Śākyamuni, the *mantra* of the dependent origination (*ye dharmā*...), the *mantras* of the Five Buddhas, followed by the *vajra*-empowerment *mantra*, and the *mantra* for the protection of the body, speech and mind.

As for the consecration of the amulets, for which a suitable place and an auspicious date should be chosen, one can follow three different formulas: long, medium, or short. Following the long formula one should first recite the preliminary invocations, take refuge and raise

---

[1] The Sanskrit *mantras* inscribed on the Drawing A have been copied from the *Rin-chen gter-mdzod* without introducing corrections. Although there are many mistakes, the intended meanings are quite clear.

the Thought of Enlightenment. Next, one offers a *gtor-ma* to the deities. The amulet is incensed and the obstructive spirits (*bgegs*) are pacified by sprinkling the sacred water. The deities are summoned and invited to dissolve into the mystic letter. Then they are worshipped and suitable verses of praise are recited. The amulet is consecrated by reciting *oṃ ye dharmā*[2] etc, and the *mantras* inscribed on the amulet. It should be folded evenly and without breaking the inner circle. Finally one places the amulet on the head, throat and heart reciting *Oṃ Āḥ Hūṃ Hrīh vajra-guru-deva-ḍākinī kaya-vāk-citta-adhiṣṭhana-abhi-ṣiñca mam.*

The medium length formula consists of generating the deities, summoning and inviting them to remain in the amulet. Their appropriate *mantras* are recited twenty one times and flowers are offered to them. Next the consecration formula is recited. Finally the protective deities of the one for whom the amulet is made are envisaged and their appropriate rites are performed.

The short formula consists of generating the deities and the protective entourage, incensing the amulet and reciting the consecration formula.

---

[2] *Oṃ ye dharmā hetuprabhavā hetuṃ teṣāṃ tathagāto āha // teṣāṃ ca yo nirodho evaṃ vādī mahāśramaṇaḥ //* — Whatever events originate from a cause, their (primary) cause was explained by the *Tathāgata*. Also their final cessation was declared by the Great Ascetic.

A. An example of a fully drawn amulet
(*srung-ba*)

---

[3] Whenever the material on which the mantras are inscribed is not specified here in the descriptions, the *bla-ma* who make the amulets follow their own tradition. Generally they use the Tibetan paper or silk. When the manner of wearing the amulets is not specified in the text, the people who wear them generally fasten them about their necks.

[4] This refers to the five colours of the Five Buddhas: white, blue, red, yellow and green.

[5] These are: nutmeg, cloves, saffron, cardamom, camphor, and sandalwood.

1. Amulet against the harm caused by the eight classes of spirits (*sde-brgyad*).

It is drawn with vermillion or gold or some other thing[3] and wrapped with five kinds of silk.[4]

Mantra: Protect the one who wears this against the harm caused by the eight classes of spirits.

2. Amulet against contamination and impurity (*grib dang mi gtsang*).

It is drawn on white silk and smeared with the six good things[5] and liquid camphor. Then it is tied on the crown of the head.

Mantra: Protect the one who wears this against all enemies who do harm to the body, speech and mind, these three.

3. Amulet against eye-diseases (*mig-nad*).

It is drawn with the liquid of white sandalwood, wrapped in snake's skin and worn about the neck.

Mantra: May all the senses of the one who wears this become clear. Protect against all eye-diseases.

4. Amulet against epidemics (*rims*).

It is drawn with pure water and smeared with liquid musk. It is worn under the left arm-pit. It is efficacious in preventing all infectious diseases; especially all kinds of epidemics become harmless.

Mantra: Protect the one who wears this against all epidemics, plagues and the rest.

5. Amulet against weapons (*mtshon*).

It is drawn with the blood of a man killed with a knife and inserted into a pouch made of red silk. While worn it should adhere to the warmth of the body and it should not be seen by other men.

Mantra: Protect and defend the one who wears this against all kinds of weapons, such as arrows, spears, swords and so forth.

6. Amulet against the wrathful deities (*lha-khros*).

It is drawn with saffron on a clean piece of cloth or on fine birch-bark and smeared with water mixed with saffron.

Mantra: Protect the body, speech, and mind, these three, of the one who wears this against all injuries and harms of the wrathful deities.

7. Amulet against the harm caused by snakes (*klu*).

It is drawn on silk or cotton or birch-bark, whichever is available, and smeared with liquid consisting of musk, pure water and incense. It is wrapped in frog's skin and worn on the body.

Mantra: Protect the body, speech and mind, these three, of the one who wears this against all harms caused by snakes. Protect against all snake-venom.

8. Amulet against the harm caused by local deities (*sa-bdag*).

It is drawn with a mixture of Indian ink and the blood of a man killed with a knife in the prime of his life. It is wrapped together with a *phur-pa* four fingers big and made of drift-wood.

Mantra: Protect the body, speech and mind, these three, of the one who wears this against all harms caused by local deities.

9. Amulet preventing the spreading of leprosy (*mdze-'phro*).

It is drawn with the blood of a leprous man, placed inside a tortoise[6] and worn on the body.

Mantra: Protect the body, speech and mind, these three, of the one who wears this. Avert leprosy! Prevent the spreading of leprosy!

---

[6] Normally the people who make the amulets use only small particles of bones, skin etc, and not the whole as the text seems to suggest.

10. Amulet against the harm caused by *yakshas* (*gnod-sbyin*).

It is drawn on white silk and placed together with the five jewels[7] inside a pouch made from the skin of a *sre-mo*[8].

Mantra: Protect the one who wears this from all injuries of the *yakshas*. Increase continually fame, wealth and enjoyment.

11. Amulet against the harm caused by she-demons (*ma-mo*).

Over this amulet and seven grains of white mustard one recites twenty-eight times saying: *bhyo ma ma ru lu ru lu dun a tir rakshaṃ*. One wraps it in black silk or black woollen cloth, and wears it on the body.

Mantra: Protect the body, speech and mind, these three, of the one who wears this against all harms caused by she-demons. Give protection!

12. Amulet against the harm caused by *rakshasas* (*srin-po*).

It is drawn with the blood of a spotted goat and worn on the body.

Mantra: Protect the one who wears this against all harms and injuries caused by *rakshasas*.

13. Amulet against the harm caused by a dead person who has become a *'dre* (*gshin-'dre*).

It is drawn with ink mixed with liquid consisting of saffron, musk, and sandalwood. It is worn on the body.

Mantra: Protect the body, speech and mind, these three, of the one who wears this against the harm caused by a dead person who has become a *'dre*.

14. Amulet against the harm caused by quarrelsome demons (*the'u-rang*).

It is tied on the body together with nine kinds of wood, namely white cotton, juniper, aloe, acacia, turmeric, black thorn-bush, rose-tree, 'rock-shrab', and tamarisk.

Mantra: Protect the body, speech and mind, these three, of the one who wears this against the harm caused by quarrelsome demons.

15. Amulet against the harm caused by female *'dre* (*mo-'dre*).

It is tied with the hair of a whore, wrapped in a woollen cloth of black colour, and worn under the left arm-pit.

Mantra: Protect the body, speech and mind, these three, of the one who wears this against all harms caused by female *'dre*.

16. Amulet for procuring procreation (*srid-spel*).

It is wrapped in a silk cloth together with a pregnant cowrie which is without spots or holes. It is tied on women's bodies.

Mantra: I beg an increase of life. I beg for *siddhi* (attainment) of life.

17. Amulet for procuring a male offspring.

It is wrapped together with a seed of the *bodhi-tsi* tree in a piece of a clean garment of a woman who has given birth to seven sons. It is tied on the body of a woman who desires a son.

Mantra: Produce a male offspring for the woman who wears this; the *siddhi* of a son *Hūṃ*.

18. Amulet against a living female *'dre* (*gson 'dre-mo*).

It is drawn with vermillion on a tablet one inch wide and made of acacia wood. While drawing it one pronounces *kshyam*. It is worn on the body.

Mantra: Protect the body, speech and mind, these three, of the one who wears this against the living female *'dre*.

19. Amulet against a living male *'dre* (*gson 'dre-pho*).

It is wrapped in a red woollen cloth together with a sword made of turmeric, one inch in size and blessed with the syllables *rNri Tri Jaḥ* inscribed on it with poisoned blood.

Mantra: Protect the body, speech and mind, these three, of the one who wears this against all those who do harmful and injurious acts of living male *'dre*.

20. Amulet against the 'ghosts' of men killed with a knife (*pho-shi gri-po*).

It is drawn with ink mixed with the blood of a man killed with a knife in the prime of his life. Then it is wrapped in a cotton shroud together with a filing from a knife. It is worn on the body.

Mantra: Protect the body, speech and mind, these three, of the one who wears this against all the harmful and injurious acts of the 'ghosts' of men killed with a knife.

21. Amulet against the 'ghosts' of women killed with a knife (*mo-shi gri-mo*).

It is wrapped together with a small red stone taken from a cemetery in which a woman has died.

Mantra: Protect the body, speech and mind, these three, of the one who wears this against all harmful and injurious acts of the 'ghosts' of women killed with a knife.

22. Amulet against mountain *'dre* (*ri-'dre*).

It is wound up with the hair of a living hare.

Mantra: Protect the body, speech and mind, these three, of the one who wears this against all harms of the mountain *'dre*.

23. Amulet against the *'dre* who cause leprosy (*mdze-'dre*).

It is written on a poisoned paper with the blood of a leper or smeared with his urine. It is worn on the body.

Mantra: Protect the body, speech and mind, these three, of the one who wears this against all harms of the *'dre* who cause leprosy.

24. Amulet against the harm caused by *btsan*.

It is wrapped together with the right claw of a fine cock in a pouch made of a red woollen and cotton cloth.

Mantra: Protect the one who wears this against all harms caused by *btsan*.

25. Amulet against the harm caused by the planet *Rahu* (*drang-srong gza'*).

It is drawn on a red piece of silk with ink and the six good things, would up with threads of five different colours and worn about the neck.

Mantra: Protect the one who wears this against all harms of the planet *Rahu*.

26. Amulet against all spirits (*'byung-po*).

It is wound up with threads of five different colours and tied on the body together with the blade of an iron-knife with nine little holes.

Mantra: Protect the body, speech and mind, these three, of the one who wears this against all harms caused by the spirits.

27. Amulet against the harm caused by *rgyal-'gong*.

In the middle of this amulet one places incense and flesh of a person killed with a knife. It is wrapped with strips of monkey's hide or wound up with its hair.

Mantra: Protect the body, speech and mind, these three, of the one who wears this against all harms caused by *rgyal-'gong*.

28. Amulet against the harm caused by woman-ghosts (*bsen-mo*).

It is wound up with the hair of a black dog and fastened with a thread made of the hair combed from a widower.

Mantra: Protect the body, speech and mind, these three, of the one who wears this against all harms caused by woman-ghosts.

29. Amulet against the harm of *bse-rag*, the hunger-devil (*lto-'dre*).

It is smeared with candied sugar mixed with the liquid of gall-stone and red sandalwood. It is worn on the body.

Mantra: Protect the body, speech and mind, these three, of the one who wears this against all harms of hunger-devils. Grant the *siddhi* of an increased appetite.

30. Amulet protecting against the harm caused by human plagues (*mi-yams*).

It is folded inside a tablet made of juniper tree and worn on the body.

Mantra: Protect the body, speech and mind, these three, of the one who wears this against all harms caused by human plagues.

31. Amulet against the harm caused by *dam-sri*.

It is smeared with incense and wound up with a black thread spun by an accomplished *mantrin*.

Mantra: Protect the body, speech and mind, these three, of the one who wears this against all harms caused by *dam-sri*.

32. Amulet against all evils of pollution (*grib-gnon*).

It is drawn with the blood of men and women whose family lineage has been broken, smeared with poisoned liquid and worn around the neck.

Mantra: Protect the body, speech and mind, these three, of the one who wears this against all harms caused by the evil of pollution.

33. Amulet against the harm caused by 'evil spells' (*gtad*).

It is placed inside a pouch made from a shroud together with a *phurpa* made of acacia wood, turmeric or black thorn, whichever available, one inch big and covered with paint.

Mantra: Protect the one who wears this against the harms caused by 'evil spells'. May the harms caused by the hidden 'evil spells' become pacified.

34. Amulet against the harm caused by demons of the upper spheres (*ya-bdud*).

It is drawn on a bark and wrapped with silk of five colours. It is worn on the body.

Mantra: Protect the one who wears this against the harm caused by demons of the upper spheres.

35. Amulet against the harm caused by demons of the lower spheres (*ma-bdud*).

It is wrapped inside a pouch made of felt produced from the hair of a black cow. It is smeared with the black rush and the callus of a black horse, and worn on the body.

Mantra: Protect the one who wears this against all harms caused by demons of the lower spheres.

36. Amulet against the flesh-eating *dakinis*.

It is drawn with the menstrual blood of a widow and wrapped in a black shroud.

Mantra: Protect the one who wears this against the flesh-eating *dakinis* and all harms and fears of *dakinis*.

37. Amulet against the harm caused by *gnyan*.

It is either drawn or smeared with the liquid prepared from scent, musk and garlic extract.

Mantra: Protect the one who wears this against *gnyan*. Suppress them and give protection.

38. Amulet against burning at the hearth (*thab-gzhob*).

It is drawn with the blood of a blacksmith and wrapped with a piece of blacksmith's old bellows.

Mantra: Protect the one who wears this against the harm of burning at the hearth.

39. Amulet against the soil *srin* (*sa-srin*).

It is wrapped with marmot's skin together with a piece of black scorpion's carcass.

Mantra: Protect the one who wears this against the harm caused by the soil *srin*.

40. Amulet against the pasture *srin* (*'brog-srin*).

It is drawn with the blood of a white grouse and wrapped with the skin of a suitable wild animal.

Mantra: Protect the one who wears this against the harm caused by the pasture *srin*.

41. Amulet against painful ulcers (*lhog-gzer*).

It is drawn with the liquid prepared from black sulphur, musk and callus of a black horse. It is smeared with ochre water, wrapped with snake's skin, and worn on the body.

Mantra: Protect the one who wears this against the harm caused by painful ulcers.

42. Amulet against the displeasure of the hearth-god *(thab-mkhon)*.

It is drawn with the blood of a spotted goat, wrapped with otter's skin, and worn on the body.

Mantra: Protect the body, speech and mind. These three, of the one who wears this against the harm resulting from the displeasure of the hearth-god.

43. Amulet against the *sri* who cause harm to old people (*rgan-sri*).

It is inserted tightly inside a tablet made of a dead tree, and worn on the body.
Mantra: Protect the one who wears this against the *sri* who cause harm to old people.

44. Amulet against the *sri* who cause harm to young people (*gzhon-sri*).

It is drawn with the blood of a kid dead inside the womb and wrapped with monkey's skin or it is drawn with monkey's blood and wrapped with kid's skin. It is worn on the body.
Mantra: Protect the one who wears this against the *sri* who cause harm to young people.

45. Amulet against the *sri* who cause harm to people in the prime of life (*dar-sri*).

It is drawn with the blood of a man in the prime of life, fastened with the thread spun from a *mantrin's* hair and worn on the body.
Mantra: Protect the one who wears this against all harms of the *sri* who cause harm to people in the prime of life.

46. Amulet against *rGyal-po Pe-har*.

It is drawn with the blood of a white dog or when not available with the spittle, wrapped with a piece of white silk and worn on the body.

Mantra: Protect the one who wears this against all harms caused by *Pe-har*.[9]

47. Amulet against *Dam-can rDor-legs*.

It is wrapped with the membrane of a spotted goat's heart and worn on the body. One is protected against the jealousy of men and consequently against the harm of the nine *the'u-rang* brothers.

Mantra: Protect the one who wears this against the harm caused by *rDor-legs*.

48. Amulet against the thirty Leaders of the Proud Ones (*dregs-pa'i sde-dpon*).

It is drawn on black silk with the fresh blood of a very able *mantrin* and wrapped with a shroud together with the hair and finger-nails of nine men of different names and different families.

Mantra: Protect the body, speech and mind, these three, of the one who wears this against the harm caused by the thirty Leaders of the Proud Ones.

---

[9] For different spellings of the name of this protective deity see Nebesky-Wojkowitz, *Oracles and Demons of Tibet*, The Hague 1956, p.96.

49. Amulet against the eighteen Proud Masters of Spells (*sngags-dpon dregs*).

It is drawn with the blood of a black cat and wound up with the membrane of a horse's heart.

Mantra: Protect the body, speech and mind, these three, of the one who wears this against all harms caused by the eighteen Proud Masters of Spells.

50. Amulet against internal quarrels (*nang-'thab*).

It is fastened with a thread made of dog's hair and goat's wool, and wrapped with rat's skin. It is worn in turns by the master and disciples or the members of the family who continually cause disputes.

Mantra: May the two parties of this amulet, of such and such names, their evil inclinations having been purified, become friends. Protect against quarrels and grudges.

51. Amulet against the evil resulting from oaths[10] (*mna-'nyes*).

It is wrapped in a piece of garment of a man who carried many corpses, together with a rabbit's ear, a badger's tongue, and a pig's nose. It is carried in the shoe or below the waist.

Mantra: Protect the body, speech and mind, these three, of the one who wears this against the evil resulting from oaths.

---

[10] It is given to people who break or take perjurious oaths.

52. Amulet against the evil resulting from wrong activities.

It is drawn with a liquid prepared from extracts of frog, snake and scorpion. It is worn on the body together with a piece of iron-blade with nine little holes. This amulet averts evils resulting from turning the soil, digging holes, moving stones or cutting trees and similar activities which may offend various local deities.

Mantra: Protect the one who wears this from wrong ways in his works.

53. Amulet against poison.

It is drawn with peacock's blood and wrapped with monkey's stomach together with rabbit's mouth. It is worn about the neck.

Mantra: Protect the one who wears this against the harm of poison.

54. Amulet against all human diseases (*mi-nad-kun*).

It is drawn with the liquid of crushed lead mixed with the urine of a dog scared by a '*dre*.[11] It is attached on the body by the master of the household and it should be done during the winter time.

Mantra: Protect these people in their houses, thresholds, roads and lanes against all harms of many different diseases.

---

[11] It is believed that when dogs see a '*dre* they howl.

55. Amulet against inauspicious dreams (*rmi-lam ngan-pa*).

It is drawn with the tears of a man who has encountered a *'dre*, wound up evenly with his eyelids, passed through the hands of nine men of different names and different families, and tied on the body.

Mantra: Protect the one who wears this against the harm of inauspicious dreams.

May evil dreams affect enemies.

56. Amulet against bad omens (*ltas ngan-pa*).

It is drawn with owl's blood, wrapped with monkey's skin, and enveloped with fox's skin.

Mantra: Protect so and so (name is written) who wears this against all harms caused by inauspicious omens.

57. Amulet against evil machinations (*sems-sbyor ngan-pa*).

It is drawn with the ink prepared from hail-water and snot and spittle of a *mantrin*, inserted inside a wooden tablet which has been poisoned, and worn on the body.

Mantra: Protect the one who wears this against all evil machinations of his enemies.

58. Amulet against witches and sorcerers (*phra-men 'gon*).

It is drawn with the ambrosia or sacred medicine mixed with vermillion. It is worn on the head or above one's bed or inside the hat.

Mantra: Protect the one who wears this against all harms of witches and sorcerers.

59. Amulet against the harm caused by the evil of oppression (*mnan-pa*).[12]

It is drawn with scented water, wrapped in black silk together with the soil from a consecrated *chos-rten*. It is worn on the body.

Mantra: Protect the one who wears this against all harms of evil of oppression.

60. Amulet against those who split up friendships (*nye-'byed*).

It is drawn on human skin or on birch-bark which is wrapped with human skin. Whichever way it is done it is drawn with vermillion and tied on the body together with a tablet of sandalwood.

Mantra: Protect the one who wears this against all harms caused by enemies who split up friendships.

61. Amulet against the harassment of fierce activities (*bskrad-gzir*).[13]

It is written with the liquid of panned out gold, wrapped inside a silk pouch of yellow colour, and worn under the left arm-pit.

Mantra: Protect the one who wears this against the evil machinations of enemies who perform fierce activities.

62. Amulet against the obscurations caused by thousands of *lha* and *'dre*.

It is placed inside a pouch made from human skin and worn on the body. When it is affixed one should look at a big fire which is like a big conflagration of the world. One is then protected against all harms of evil *'dre*.[14]

Mantra: Suppress for the one who wears this all harms caused by the *lha* and *'dre* of the visible world.

---

[12] This amulet is worn for protection against the people who write one's name on a piece of cloth or paper together with all kinds of evil wishes and stick it in the earth.

[13] This refers to different fierce rites during which the fierce protective deities are placated to bring evil upon other people; also mustard seeds recited over with fierce *mantras* are thrown and offensive objects pointed in the direction of people upon whom one wants to bring misfortune.

[14] Once a lama told me that the best way of making this amulet is to find a piece of wood (called *sgrib-shing*) which renders one invisible to *lha* and *'dre*. Such small pieces of wood can be found in crow nests which are invisible. To be able to see the nest one should hold a dog's tail against one's eyes. Once found the nest should be thrown in a river. The whole nest will float down the stream except for a small piece of wood which will float up the stream. This piece of wood worn together with the amulet renders one invisible to *lha* and *'dre*.

63. Amulet against house thieves.

It is drawn with the blood of a great thief, wrapped with rat's skin, and attached to a pole in the tent or to a pillar in the house or any other habitation.

Mantra: Protect the one who has this against the endeavours and scheming machinations of thieves.

64. Amulet against contamination done by *sri*.

It is drawn with the semen of a man in the prime of life. Together with a tablet made of fine yellow wood, one inch in size, engraved with '*rakshyaṃ*' and smeared with rat's blood, it is placed over a barley container or some other dishes or attached to the handle of a wheat container or other suitable dishes.

Mantra: Defile the *sri* in the house and home of the bearer. Protect against bad harvest and bad *chang*.

65. Amulet against demons who cause losses (*god-kha*).

It is drawn on birch bark, smeared with vermillion or arsenic and affixed on the upper bar of the gate facing outwards.

Mantra: Protect the bearer against losses in the house, on the approach and on the path. Bring loss to the *'dre* who causes losses (*god-'dre*).

66. Amulets which cuts off the pathways of '*dre*.

It is drawn with the blood of a wolf or a dog which howls at '*dre* and a bird belonging to the family of night birds. It is affixed on a mirror and placed on the gate facing outwards.

Mantra: Protect the bearer from encountering '*dre* in the house, in the doorways and passages.

67. Amulet against the fears of fire.

It is drawn with frog's blood, placed together with a *phur-pa* made of driftwood and four fingers long inside a badger's skull and hidden in the innermost part of the house.

Mantra: Protect the bearer's house against the harm of conflagration.

68. Amulet against damages to crops.

It is wound up with the hair of a living hare, tied with a white thread spun by an unmarried and innocent girl, and wrapped with a shroud. It is attached to the jewel-top of the post in the middle of the fields.

Mantra: Protect the bearer's crops against all smut, frost, hail, insects, worms, birds, and mice.

69. Amulet against the *'dre* who torment children.

It is wrapped with the bark of a female *sre* (species of wood) and attached on the neck of a loudly crying child who is tormented by *'dre*.
Mantra: Protect the body, speech and mind, these three, of the one who wears this against the harm of *'dre* and *gdon*.

70. Amulet against tooth diseases.

It is drawn with a pure liquid prepared from garlic extract, incense and black sulphur. It is wound up with dog's hair.
Mantra: Protect the one who wears this against tooth diseases.

71. Amulet against the fears of lightning.

It is drawn with the blood from woman's womb, wrapped in widow's underwear and fastened on the body. It protects against lightning and hail storms.
Mantra: Protect the one who wears this against the harm of lightning.

72. Amulet against poisonous bites (*so-dug*).

It is drawn with a liquid of potent poison and musk, wrapped with pig's skin and worn on the body.

Mantra: Protect the body, speech and mind, these three, of the one who wears this against the harm of poisonous bites.

73. Amulet against the beasts of prey.

It is drawn with a liquid of crushed iron-blade and myrabalan, and smeared with musk-water.

Mantra: Protect the one who wears this against the harm of the beasts of prey.

74. Amulet against smallpox.

It is drawn with the liquid of black thorn and smeared with the dust rubbed off the bottom of a vase which belonged to a man who died of smallpox.

Mantra: Protect the one who wears this against smallpox. Protect against all the harm due to boils.

75. Amulet against the *'dre* who cause insanity (*smyo-'dre*).

It is drawn with Indian vermillion and wrapped with the membrane of donkey's heart.

Mantra: Protect the one who wears this against the *'dre* who causes insanity.

76. Amulet against gossip and idle talk.

It is drawn with ink prepared either from soot taken from a rest house or from a clay pot belonging to a prostitute. It is inserted inside a pouch made of rodent's skin and worn on the body.

Mantra: Protect the one who wears this against all gossip and idle talk.

77. Amulet against the harm caused by dogs.

It is drawn with leopard's blood and worn on the body together with a piece of leopard's skin.

Mantra: Protect the one who wears this against the harm caused by dogs.

78. Amulet against thieves.
It is drawn with the blood of a wolf or a wild dog, and worn on the body.
Mantra: Protect the one who wears this against the harm of enemy thieves.

79. Amulet against bandits.
It is drawn with the blood of a black dog and worn on the body.
Mantra: Protect the bearer of such and such a name and his companions against the harm of enemy bandits and robbers.

80. Amulet against sleep-talking and sleepwalking (*bla-brdol sad-langs*).
Having been drawn it is double-folded, wound up with a thread spun from widower's or widow's hair, and worn on the body.
Mantra: Protect the one who wears this against the harm of sleep-talking and sleepwalking.

81. Amulet against bandits and beasts of prey hostile to horses and cattle.

It is wrapped tightly with the hair of nine men of different names and different families. It is affixed on horses and cattle.
Mantra: Protect the horses and cattle against the harm of hostile thieves and beasts of prey.

82. Amulet preventing the flow of semen.

It is drawn with the menstrual blood of a young girl, tied with a blue and red thread spun by an unmarried and innocent girl, and tied on the body.
Mantra: Stop the flow of semen in respect of the body, speech and mind, these three, of the one who wears this.

83. Amulet against the harmful planets and stars (*gza' skar ngan-pa*).

It is drawn with ink prepared from the broken bones and ashes of a corpse of a man who died because of the harmful planets and stars.
Mantra: Protect the one who wears this against the damages of the harmful planets and stars.

84. Amulet against inauspicious dates.

It is drawn, without mistaking the date, on the fifteenth of a suitable month. It is smeared with different medicines and worn on the body.
Mantra: Protect the one who wears this against the harm of inauspicious time-periods and dates.

85. Amulet against bad places.

It is inserted inside a tablet made of the male juniper tree and the female willow tree, and worn on the body.
Mantra: Protect the one who wears this against the harm of bad places.

86. Amulet against the five *'dre*.[15]

It is either drawn or smeared with the liquid of white rush or saffron or white sandalwood, whichever is available. It is worn on the body.
Mantra: Protect the one who wears this against the harm of five *'dre*.

---

[15] The evil activities of the five *'dre* and *bdud-gcod* are detected through astrological calculations.

87. Amulet against the destructive demons (*bdud-gcod*).

It is drawn with the liquid of vermillion or a ground jewel, whichever is suitable, or it is smeared with them. It is wrapped with the silk of five colours and worn on the body.

Mantra: Protect the one who wears this against destructive demons.

88. Amulet against the water *'dre* (*chu-'dre*).

It is drawn with gold or another jewel which is available and in the centre of it one places a drop of gold.

Mantra: Protect the one who wears this against the harm of the water *'dre*.

89. Amulet against floods (*shva-sbud?*)

It is placed inside a *tsatsha* which is consecrated and placed inside a heap of yellow stones at the place where a flood has happened.

Mantra: Protect the bearer against the harm of floods. Avert them!

90. Amulet against the *'dre* who follow behind.

This amulet and the people who suffer from *'dre* who follow behind are first fumigated with the smoke produced from incense (*gu-gul*), the flesh of a great sinner and Chinese paper. Next it is attached on the body.

Mantra: Protect the one who wears this against the *'dre* who walk ahead (*gdong-'re*). accompany (*'grul-rngur?*) and follow behind (*'gab 'dre*).[16]

91. Amulet against abscesses, lameness and rheumatism.

It is attached on the bodies of those who suffer from abscesses, skin diseases, rheumatism etc.

Mantra: Protect the one who wears this against all kinds of unhappiness.

---

[16] These three kinds of *'dre* do not follow or accompany the person who suffers from them but the person who brings them. If some accident happens in a house or a person becomes ill before a stranger arrives in the house it is called *gdong-'dre*. When something bad happens after a stranger has left it is called *'gab-'dre*, etc.

92. Amulet for producing long life (*tshe-srog*).[17]

It is affixed on those whose life force is impaired. It protects against the harm caused to one's life.

Mantra: Protect life (-force) for the one who wears this. Prolong life. Protect against fatal accidents to life.

93. Amulet for rejuvenating the body (*lus-skyed*).

It is affixed on the bodies of old people. It rejuvenates the body and protects it from harmful influences.

Mantra: Produce bodily strength for the one who wears this. Protect from all bodily harms.

94. Amulet for producing power (*dbang-thang*).

It is affixed on those people whose effectiveness is impaired. It increases effectiveness and protects against all harms which prevent it.

Mantra: Increase effectiveness for the one who wears this. Replenish him with happiness and wealth.

---

[17] This and the next four amulets relate to astrological calculations whereby good and evil influences of the five elements are calculated in relationship to the year of one's birth.

95. Amulet for producing good luck (*klung-rta*).

This amulet which produces the wind-horse (*rlung-rta*) and from which all attainments come is attached on the body of the one whose wind-horse has become weak; one's good luck diffuses and one is protected against all harms caused to one's good luck.
Mantra: Diffuse good luck and make it many-fold for the one who wears this. Increase merit.

96. Amulet which accomplishes aspirations (*don-gnyer*).

This amulet which produces attainments and increases desired wealth is affixed on the body at the time of exertion in a particular place.
Mantra: May all possible aspirations of the one who wears this be accomplished according to his wishes.

97. Amulet producing success in trading.

This amulet of *Dākini Lag-'gul* (shaky hand) is affixed at the time of going for trading. One is the winner in trade and is protected from being the loser.
Mantra: May the one who wears this become successful in every kind of trading in which he is involved.

98. Amulet producing victory.

It is carried on the crown of the head by the army commander. The army comes out victorious in the battle and is protected against defeat.

Mantra: May the army commander who carries this be victorious in the battle.

99. Amulet for increasing wealth.

It is kept together with the five kinds of jewels. It increases wealth and protects against the *'dre* who bring poverty.

Mantra: Bestow upon the one who carries this the *siddhi* of enjoying wealth. Protect against the harm of *'dre* who bring poverty (*dbul-'dre*).

100. Amulet for increasing food and drink.

It brings the *siddhi* of food and drink, and protects against the harm of *'dre* who cause hunger (*ltog-'dre*).

Mantra: Bestow upon the one who wears this the *siddhi* of enjoying food and drink. Protect against the harm of *'dre* who cause hunger.

101. Amulet for producing hats and clothes.

This amulet of light with ornaments is wrapped with many kinds of silk and attached on the body of the one who is not endowed with the *siddhi* of hats and clothes. It brings those things and protects against the harm resulting from not having them.
Mantra: Protect the one of such and such a name against the fear of cold. Bestow the *siddhi* of hats and clothes.

102. Amulet for popularity.

This amulet, beautiful and adorned, is drawn with red soil and vermillion on silk and poppies. The one who wears it is liked by all living beings and all give him friendly advice.
Mantra: May the one who wears this, being pleasing to all living beings, be surrounded by kindness.

103. Amulet against the one hundred thousand *lha* and *'dre*.

It is drawn with the blood of a man, a horse and a dog, a wrapped in vulture's skin. The one who wears this amulet is protected against the harm of *dri-za, grul-bum, lto-'phye* etc.
Mantra: Protect the one who wears this against all *dri-za, grul-bum, lto-'phye* etc., the spirits under the earth, on and above the earth.

104. The fire-*cakra* protecting against the wind illnesses[18] (*rlung-nad*).

This *cakra* of steadiness is affixed together with the bones of a dog, a dragon, a bull and a sheep.[19]

Mantra: Protect the one who wears this against the harm of agitation and unsteadiness.

105. The water-*cakra* protecting against the heat.

It is drawn with the liquid of camphor and musk.

Mantra: Protect the one who wears this against the harm of heat.

106. The *cakra* protecting against the cold.

This *cakra* of burning fire is drawn with the liquid prepared from three grasses.

Mantra: Protect the one who wears this against all harms resulting from cold and wind.

---

[18] According to Tibetan medicine different winds circulate in the human body. Any disorder or malfunctioning of the winds produces various illnesses.

[19] These are the four animals which on the astrological charts are positioned towards the cardinal directions and are said to synchronize the different forces of nature.

107. The wind-*cakra* against mental inertness and dullness (*rmugs 'thib*).
The wind-*cakra* which produces movement is wrapped with green silk.
Mantra: Protect the one who wears this against the harm of drowsiness and mental dullness.

108. The *cakra* comprising all the elements.
It is wrapped with five kinds of silk and worn about the neck. It harmonizes the powers of the five elements and prevents them from causing harm.
Mantra: Protect the one who wears this against the unbalance of the five elements. Protect against the harm resulting from the disturbance of the five elements.

109. Amulet for self-protection.
It is drawn with the six good things, wrapped with five kinds of silk and fastened on one's body. One is protected while making the 108 amulets described above. It is of great importance that it should be made first.
Mantra: Protect me the yogin against all harms which come from the amulets which turn against oneself.[20]

---

[20] It is believed that when a *bla-ma* performs a ritual or makes an amulet for averting demons or evil forces he must protect himself against them. If he is unprotected, demons and evil forces might turn against him.

ONE HUNDRED AND TWO PROTECTIVE *CAKRAS*

This group of one hundred and two protective *cakras* discovered in the red *mchod-rten* at Samye is based on astrological calculations of Chinese origin whereby the time is reckoned according to the twelve-year and sixty-year cycles. The twelve-year cycle has the names of twelve animals which are:

1. Rat (*byi-ba*)
2. Ox (*glang*)
3. Tiger (*stag*)
4. Hare (*yos*)
5. Dragon (*'brug*)
6. Serpent (*shrul*)
7. Horse (*sta*)
8. Sheep (*lug*)
9. Monkey (*spre'u*)
10. Bird (*bva*)
11. Dog (*khyi*)
12. Hog (*phag*)

The sixty-year cycle is made up by combining the twelve cyclic animals with the five elements (*'byung-lnga*), namely Wood (*shing*), Fire (*me*), Earth (*sa*), Iron (*lcags*), and Water (*chu*).[1]

The astrological calculations are derived from establishing different degrees of a affinity and disagreement between the twelve cyclic animals and between the five elements which are attributed with various powers. The animals and the five elements have a number of relationships, which are considered as good or bad. The interplay of different powers attributed to the animals and the five elements produces a combination of influences which affect human life in a good or adverse manner. These various degrees of affinity

---
[1] For the description of the Tibetan calendar and astrological calculations see for example L. Austine Waddell, *Buddhism and Lamaism of Tibet*, first published in 1895, reprinted in New Delhi 1974 by Heritage Publishers, pp. 45-74.

and disagreement can be calculated in relationship to the date of one's birth, to a particular day of the week or the date of the month. As with every cyclic year, the combinations of different relationships change and one's life is affected accordingly. The protective *cakras* listed below are devised to control the bad influences and to promote the good ones, to use different influences to counteract the wicked activities of various local deities such as *sa-bdag* and others, to bring evil upon one's enemies, to protect one's property, interest, family etc, to produce prosperity and the like.

The protective *cakras* should be drawn in accordance with the drawings provided, consecrated and worn on the body, around the neck or as indicated in the descriptions. All the *mantras*, the syllables and the rest should be inscribed in printed letters. The animals should be drawn as if walking. The ceremony of consecration is done by reciting *oṃ ye dharmā* etc., raising the Thought of Enlightenment, prayer to Padmasambhava and visualizing the chosen (*yi-dam*) and protective divinities. Finally they should be incensed, folded and wound up with threads of five different colours.

1. The *cakra* of the three spells (=*Oṃ Āḥ Hūṃ*), also known as the *cakra* of the gods, is designed to bring benefit to those who are involved in performing different activities. The centre of the diagram is inscribed in Tibetan and reads: 'Protect me the bearer of the three spells'. In the four corners of the square are written the names of four animals, namely sheep, dog, ox and dragon. These four animals are known collectively in Tibetan astrology as *gshed-bzhi*—'the four fighters'. They are placed to the four corners of the calendar charts, playing thus an important role in controlling the cardinal positions. The first and second circumferences are inscribed with Sanskrit spells, but in Tibetan script, and the outer circumference with the *mantra* of dependent origination.

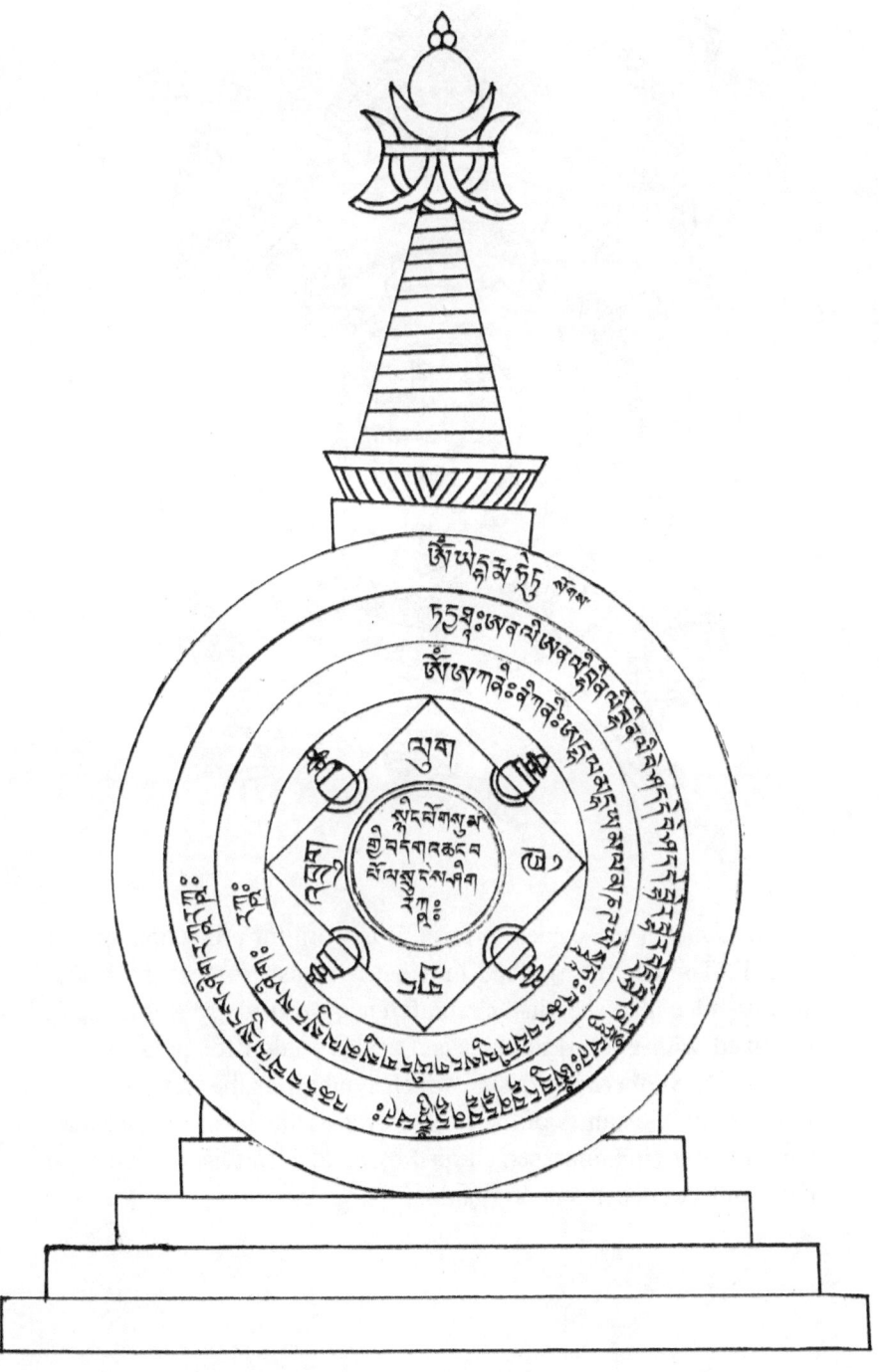

2. The *cakra* of the golden tortoise. It is worn for protection against all evil. The centre inscribed in Tibetan reads: 'Protect the bearer against all evil'. The first circumference grasped by a tortoise is inscribed with a Sanskrit spell and an invocation for protection in Tibetan. Next, there is a design which symbolizes the water element followed by the names of the twelve cyclic animals of the calendar. On the outer circumference clasped by another tortoise, is inscribed the *mantra* of dependent origination.

FIVE *CAKRAS* OF THE FIVE ELEMENTS

3. The *cakra* of the water elements. It should be worn by those born in the tiger and hare years and whose life-force (*srog*) is impeded by adverse forces. The centre of this *cakra* inscribed with the syllable *Nrih* is encircled by an invocation which reads: 'Protect the bearer'. In the four corners of the square is inscribed the syllable *Kham*. Outside the square on the four sides is inscribed: 'Protect!' Then follows the circumference inscribed with three spells in Sanskrit and an invocation in Tibetan. The next circumference is inscribed with the *mantra* of dependent origination, and the outer one has a symbolic design of the water element.

4. The *cakra* of the wood element. It should be worn by those who are born in the horse and serpent years and whose life-force is impeded by adverse forces. The centre of this *cakra* is inscribed with the same invocation as the previous one. Next, there is a lotus with eight petals in the centre of which are symbolic designs of the wood element. The circumference that follows the lotus is inscribed with two spells in Sanskrit and an invocation for protection in Tibetan. The next circumference is inscribed with the *mantra* of dependent origination and the outer one has designs of the wood element.

5. The *cakra* of the fire element. It should be worn by those born in the years of the 'four fighters' (=ox, dog, dragon, sheep) and whose life-force is impeded by adverse forces. The centre is inscribed with an invocation for protection and in the corners of the square the seed-syllable of the fire-element is inscribed twice. The first circumference is inscribed with a Sanskrit spell and an invocation for protection in Tibetan, followed by the next circumference with the *mantra* of dependent origination. The outer portion has the symbolic design of the fire element.

6. The *cakra* of the earth element. It should be worn by those born in the bird and monkey years and whose life-force is impeded by adverse forces. The centre is inscribed with the same invocation for protection as the previous *cakras*. Next there is a stylized crossed *vajra* inscribed with the syllables *Bhruṃ* and *Laṃ*, followed by two spells in Sanskrit and an invocation for protection in Tibetan. The next circumference is inscribed with the *mantra* of dependent origination and the outer part of the diagram has the symbolic design of the earth element.

7. The *cakra* of the iron element. It should be worn by those born in the rat and hog years and whose life-force is impeded by adverse forces. The centre is inscribed with the syllable *Nri* encircled by an invocation for protection. The four corners of the square are inscribed with the syllable *Kam* and on the four sides of it is written *Raksha* (=Protect!). Then follows a spell in Sanskrit and the *mantra* of dependent origination. The outer part has the symbolic design of the iron element.

FIVE *CAKRAS* OF THE TORTOISE AND THE FIVE ELEMENTS

The *cakras* of this group are grasped by tortoises. Their centres are inscribed with invocations for protection, followed by squares, an eight petalled lotus or a trapezoid-like design inscribed with spells in Sanskrit. The *mantra* of dependent origination is the outermost of all the inscriptions. The designs of the appropriate elements are drawn either inside or on the outer parts of the diagrams.

8. The *cakra* of the tortoise and the wood element. It is worn by those born in the tiger and hare years if harm is caused by the earth element.

9. The *cakra* of the tortoise and the fire element. It is worn by those born in the horse and serpent years if harm is caused by the iron element.

10. The *cakra* of the tortoise and the earth element. It is worn by those born in the years of the 'four fighters' if harm is caused by the water element.

11. The *cakra* of the tortoise and the iron element. It is worn by those born in the bird and monkey years if harm is caused by the wood element.

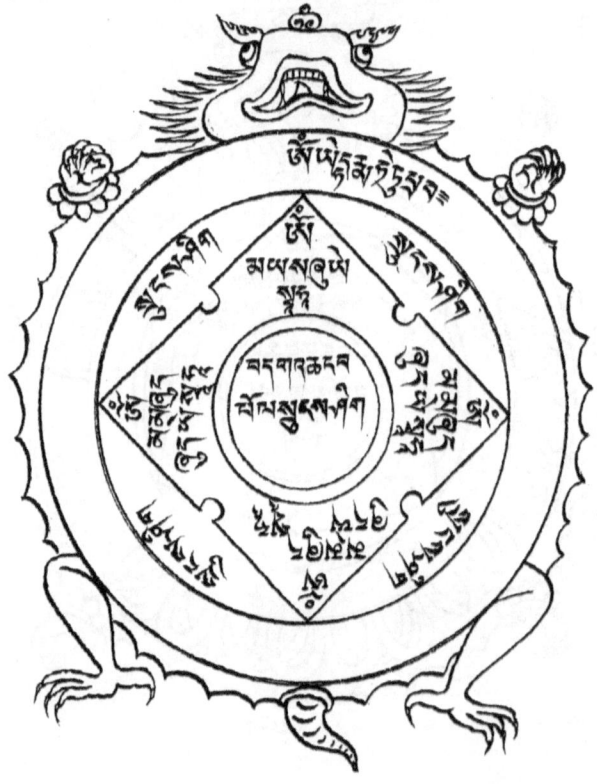

12. The *cakra* of the tortoise and the water element. It is worn by those born in the rat and hog years if harm is caused by the fire element.

FIVE *CAKRAS* AGAINST THE HARM CAUSED BY THE FIVE ELEMENTS

The five *cakras* of this group are designed in such a way so as to bring into opposition two disagreeing elements in order to diminish bad influences of the element which affects one's life in an adverse manner. The centres of the *cakras* are inscribed with the syllables *Oṃ*, *Āḥ* and *Hūṃ*, and an invocation for protection. In the four corners of the squares are inscribed the names of the element and the cyclic animals that are paired with it. The names of the element and the animals are those which stand in direct disagreement with the element against which the *cakra* is designed. Thus the *cakra* No. 13 should be inscribed with the name of the iron element (*lcags*) and two animals which go with it, namely monkey and bird. The *cakra* No. 14 is inscribed with the names of the water element, rat and hog; No. 15 with the wood element, tiger and hare; No. 16 with the fire element, dragon and horse; and the No. 17 with the earth element, and the 'four fighters' (= ox, dog, dragon, sheep). On the four sides of the squares is inscribed *Raksha* (= Protect!). Next are inscribed the names of the twelve cyclic animals followed by the names of different categories of a particular element. The outer circumferences are inscribed with the *mantra* of dependent origination.

13. The *cakra* of the six irons. It is worn if harm is caused by the wood element.

14. The *cakra* of the six waters. It is worn when harm is caused by the fire element.

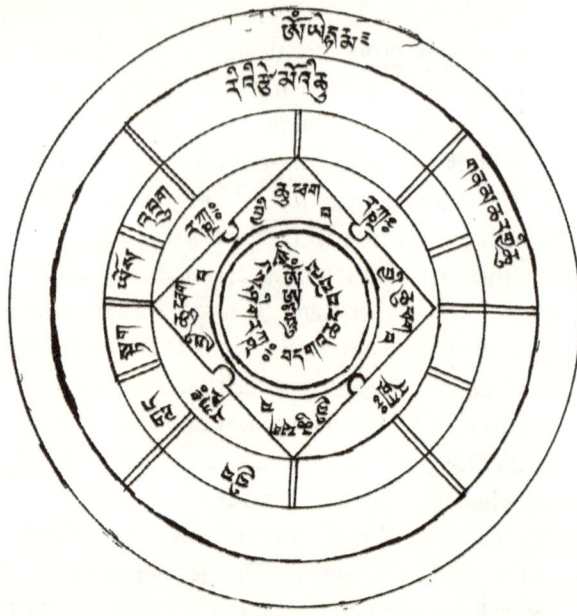

15. The *cakra* of the six woods. It is worn when harm is caused by the earth element.

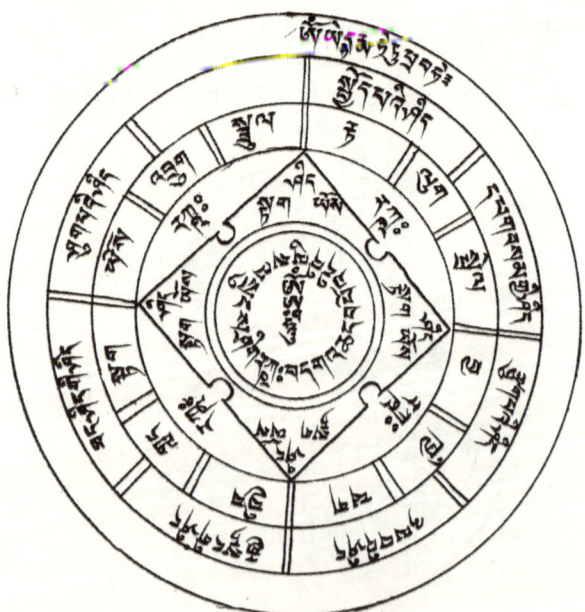

16. The *cakra* of the six fires. It is worn when harm is caused by the iron element.

17. The *cakra* of the six earths. It is worn when harm is caused by the water element.

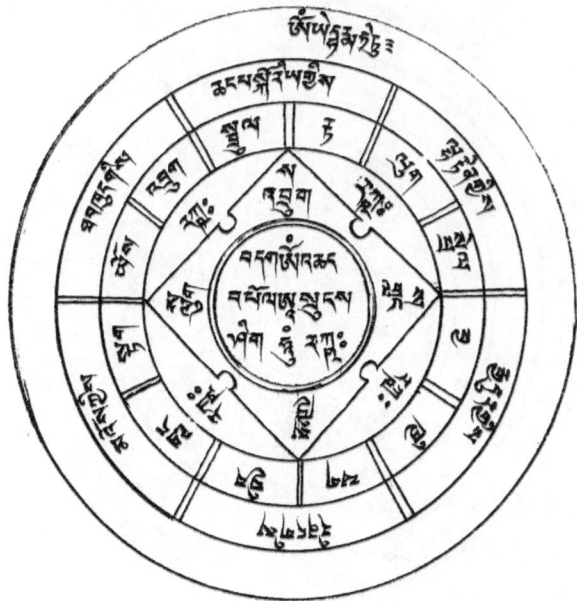

FOUR *CAKRAS* FOR CONTROLLING ADVERSE FORCES TO ONE'S LIFE (*SROG*), BODY (*LUS*), EFFECTIVENESS (*DBANG-THANG*), AND GOOD LUCK (*KLUNG-RTA*)

These *cakras* are designed to control bad influences of the five elements in relationship to the year of one's birth. Astrological calculations are made every year for the whole cycle of sixty years and written in the calendar. The positive influences for each aspect of one's life are marked with little circles and the negative ones with crosses. Life-force (*srog*) refers to the period of one's existence in one single life-time. A combination of bad influences of the five elements can shorten the period of one's life. Similarly adverse forces of one or two elements can cause accidents or illnesses which will damage one's health or body. *dBang-thang* or effectiveness refers to the powers of the five elements which influence one's performance as an individual, and *klung-rta* refers to their influence on one's good luck.

18. The *cakra* with a crossed *vajra*. It is worn when one's life-force is impeded by adverse forces.

19. The *cakra* with eight spokes. It is worn when one's body is affected by evil forces.

20. The *cakra* with *svastika* designs. It is worn when one's effectiveness is impeded by adverse forces.

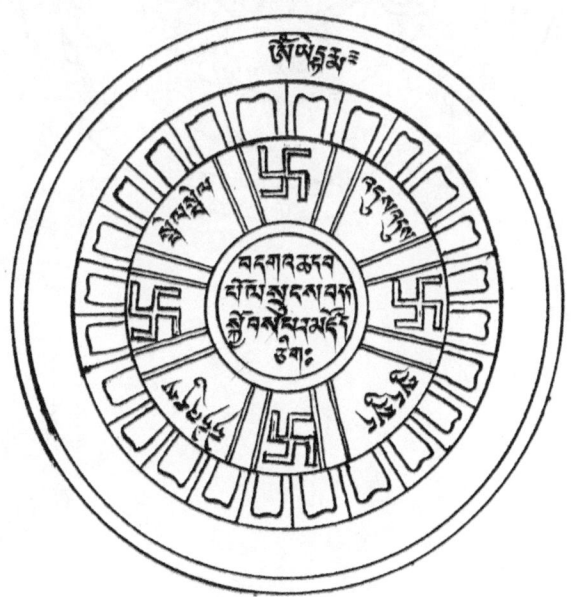

21. The *cakra* with a powerful lotus. It is worn when one's good luck is impeded by adverse forces.

FIVE *CAKRAS* WORN DURING THE PERFORMANCE OF DETRIMENTAL WORK

22. The *cakra* of the fire and hatchets. It is worn for protection against tree-spirits when cutting down trees.

23. The *cakra* of the earth and water designs. It is worn when performing *homa* rituals and cremating corpses.

24. The *cakra* of the iron and *phur-ba*. It is worn when digging the earth for protection against soil-spirits.

25. The *cakra* of the wood and eight-petalled lotus. It is worn when digging wells and ponds.

26. The *cakra* of the water and fire designs. It is worn when breaking rocks for protection against rock-spirits.

FIVE *CAKRAS* FOR PROTECTION AGAINST DIFFERENT DEMONS

27. The *cakra* with a crossed *vajra*. It is worn when harm is caused by *Pe-har*.

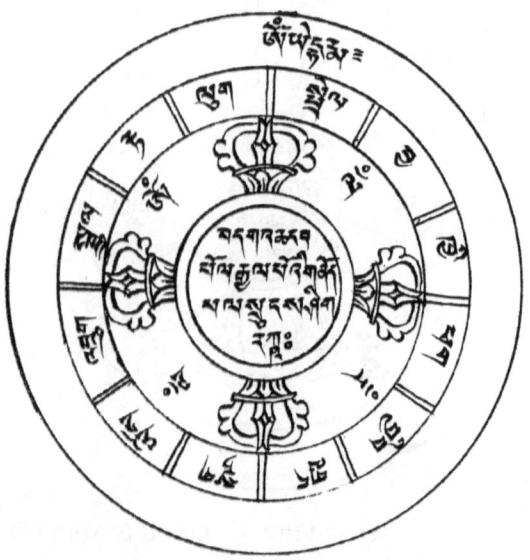

28. The *cakra* with eight petals and the syllable *Raṃ*. It is worn when harm is caused by *sa-bdag, klu* and *gnyan*.

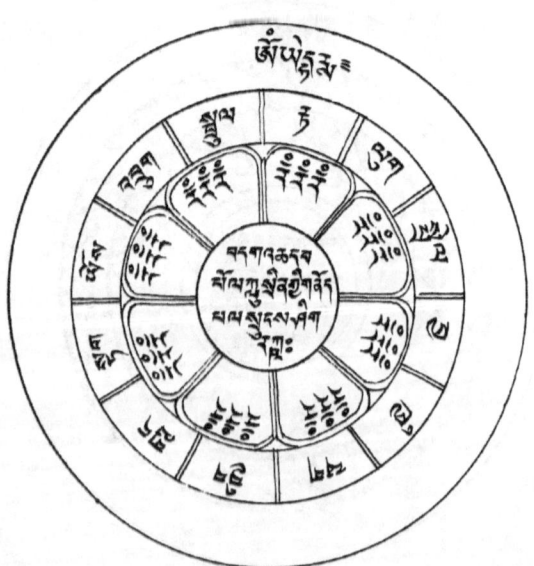

29. The *cakra* with eight spokes and the syllable *Bam*. It is worn when harm is done by *sa-bdag*, *klu* and *gnyan*.

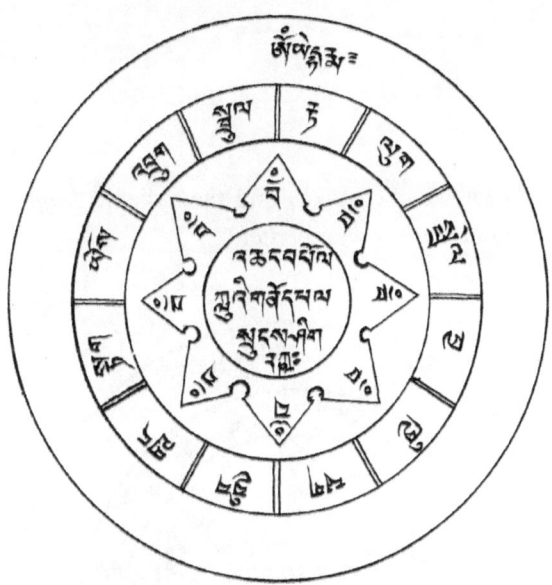

30. The *cakra* with eight spokes and the syllable *Laṃ*. It is worn when harm is caused by the demons of lower spheres (*ma-bdud*).

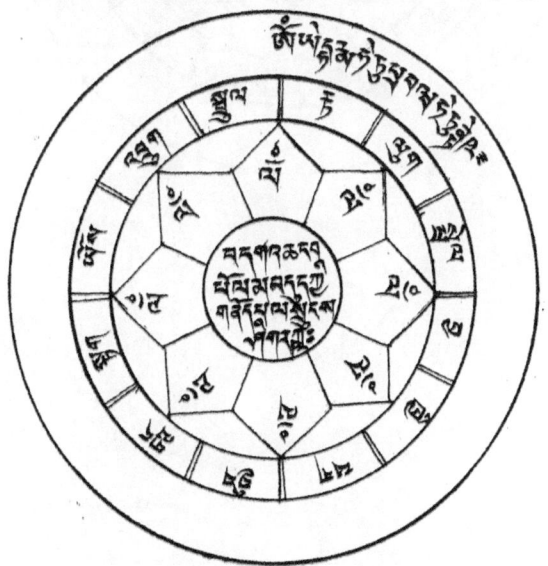

31. The *cakra* with eight spokes and the syllable *Kaṃ*. It is worn when harm is done by *btsan* and *bdud*.

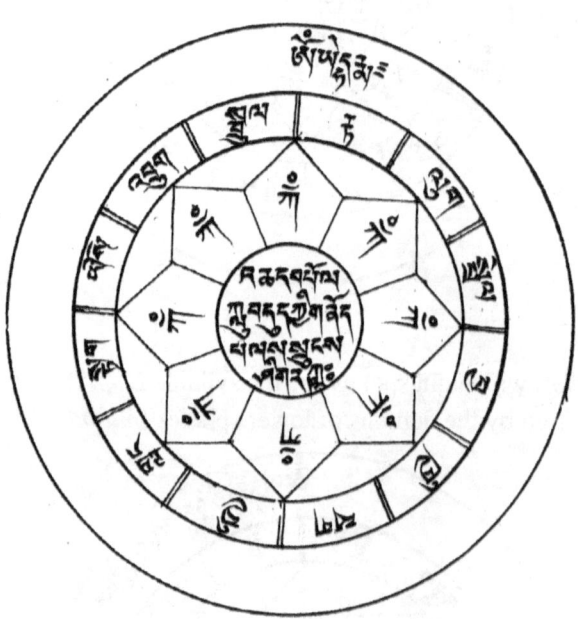

THREE *CAKRAS* OF THE PROTECTORS OF THE THREE FAMILIES (*RIGS-GSUM MGON-PO*)

32. The *cakra* of *Mañjuśrī*. It is worn when one desires wisdom.

33. The *cakra* of *Avalokiteśvara*. It is worn when one wishes to win a dispute.

34. The *cakra* of *Vajrapāṇi*. It is worn when striving for power.

TEN *CAKRAS* OF THE FIVE BUDDHAS AND FIVE BUDDHA GODDESSES

35. The *cakra* of *rNam-par snang-mdzad* (*Vairocana*). It is worn when the span of life of family lineage, people or cattle is short.

36. The *cakra* of *rDo-rje sems-dpa'* (*Vajrasattva*). It is worn at the time of many illnesses.

37. The *cakra* of *Rin-chen 'byung-ldan* (*Ratnasambhava*). It is made when continuous loss of cattle occurs.

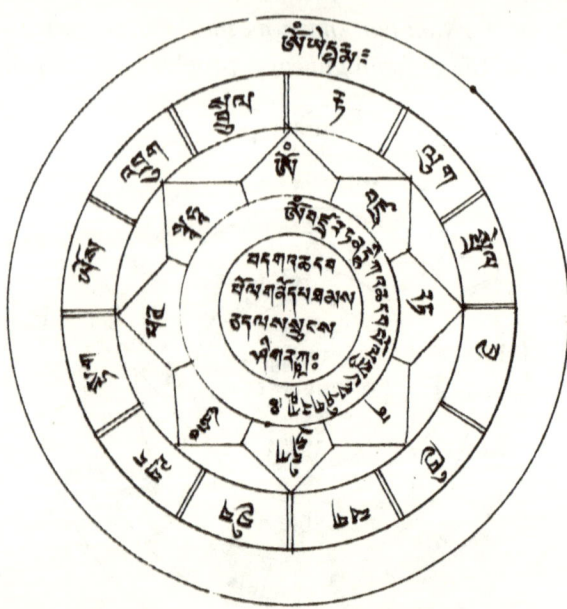

38. The *cakra* of *sNang-ba mtha'-yas* (*Amitabha*). It is worn when one is gossiped about.

39. The *cakra* of *Don-yod grub-pa* (*Amoghasiddha*). It is worn for protection against enemies and court suits.

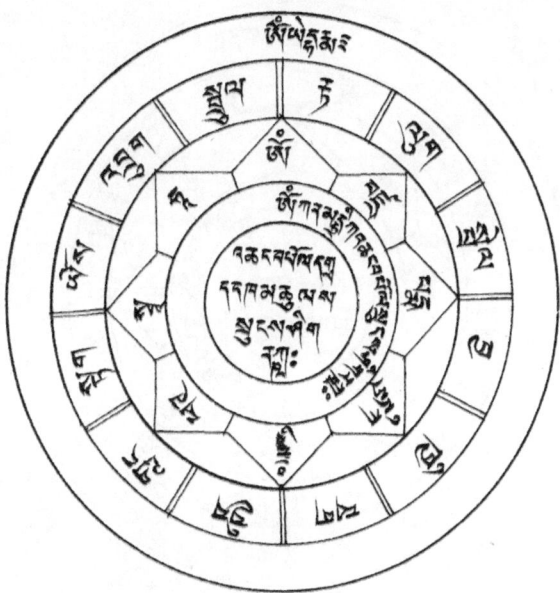

40. The *cakra* of *mKha'i dbyings-phyug* (*Dhatviśvarī*). It is worn when having bad dreams.

41. The *cakra* of *Sangs-rgyas spyan-ma* (*Locana*). It is worn when fights and quarrels arise.

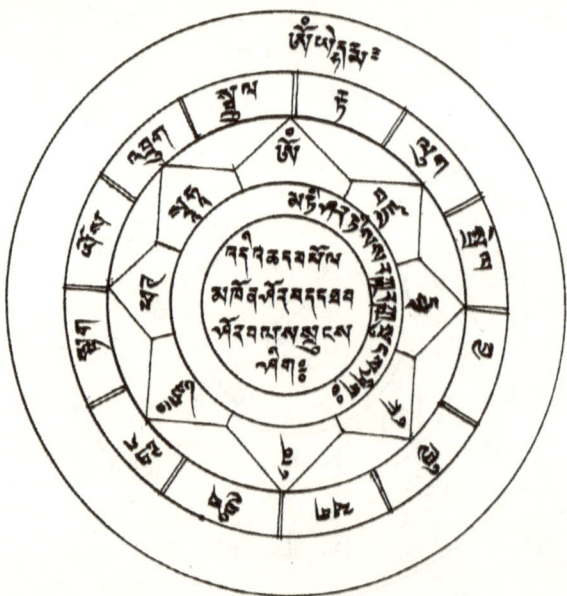

42. The *cakra* of *Māmakī*. It is worn for protection against impurities.

43. The *cakra Gos dkar-mo* (*Paṇḍuravāsinī*). It is worn against injuries at the hearth.

44. The *cakra* of *Dam-tshig sgrol-ma* (*Tārā*). It is worn when inauspicious omens occur.

TEN *CAKRAS* OF THE TEN WRATHFUL DEITIES (*KHRO-BO BCU*)

45. The *cakra* of the Wrathful *Hūṃkāra*. It is worn for protection against evil caused by demons (*gdon*).

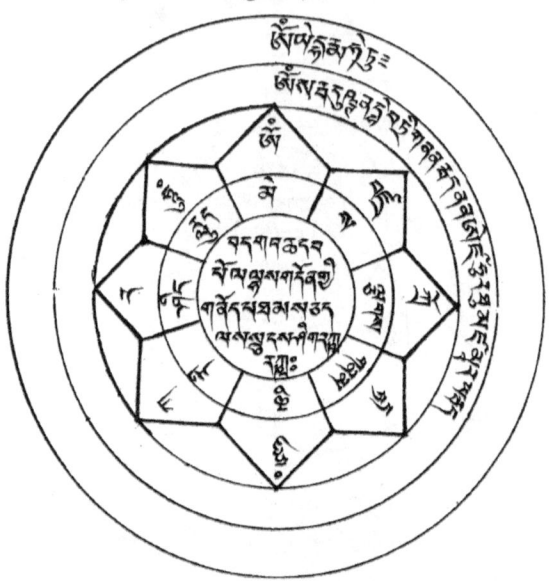

46. The *cakra* of *rNam-par rgyal-ba*. (*Vijaya*). It is worn when damages are caused by *'dre* who deprive one of wealth (*dkor-'dre*).

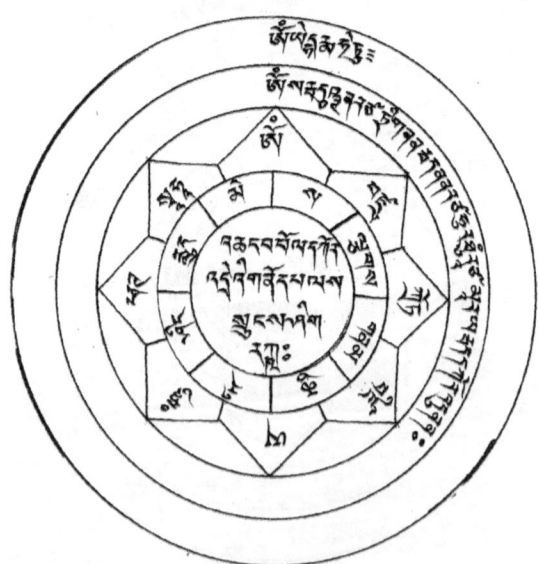

47. The *cakra* of *dByug-pa sngon-po* (*Nīladaṇḍa*). It is worn when harm is done by *btsan*.

48. The *cakra* of *gShing-rje* (*Yamāntaka*). It is worn when harm is done by *Mara's* demons.

49. The *cakra* of *Mi-g-yo mgon-po* (*Āryācala*). It is worn when harm is caused by *dam-sri*.

50. The *cakra* of *rTa-mgrin* (*Hayagrīva*). It is worn when harm is caused by *klu*.

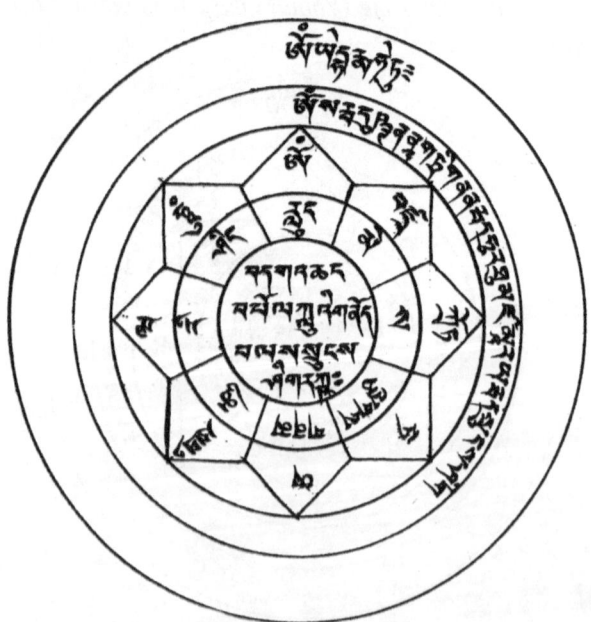

51. The *cakra* of *'Dod-pa'i rgyal-po* (*Aparacitta*). It is worn when harm is caused by *the'u-rang*.

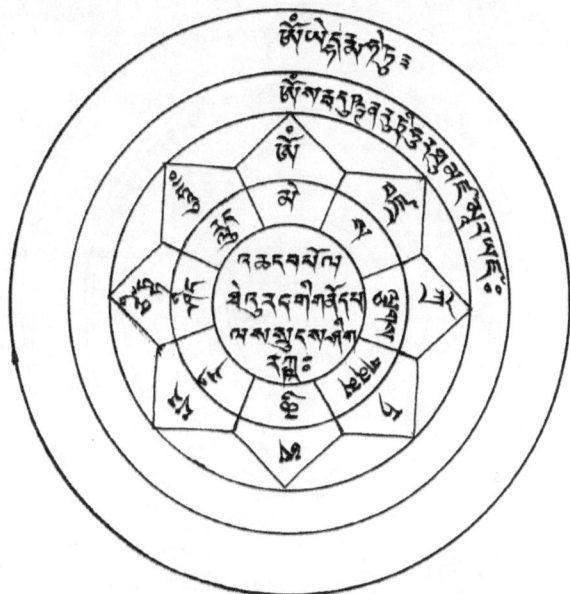

52. The *cakra* of *bDud-rtsi 'khyil-ba* (*Amrtakuṇḍali*). It is worn for protection against the *'dre* of dead people (*shi-'dre*).

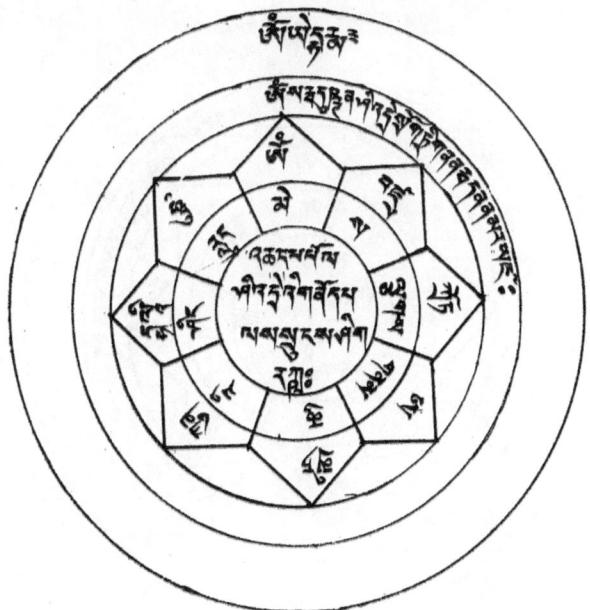

53. The *cakra* of *Khams-gsum rnam-par rgyal-ba* (*Trailokyavijaya*). It is worn when harm is caused by *bdud*.

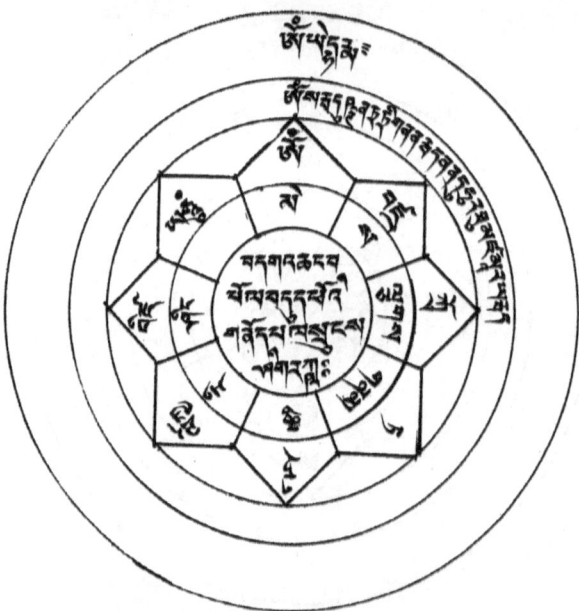

54. The *cakra* of *sTobs-po-che* (*Mahābala*). It is worn when harm is caused by *sa-bdag*.

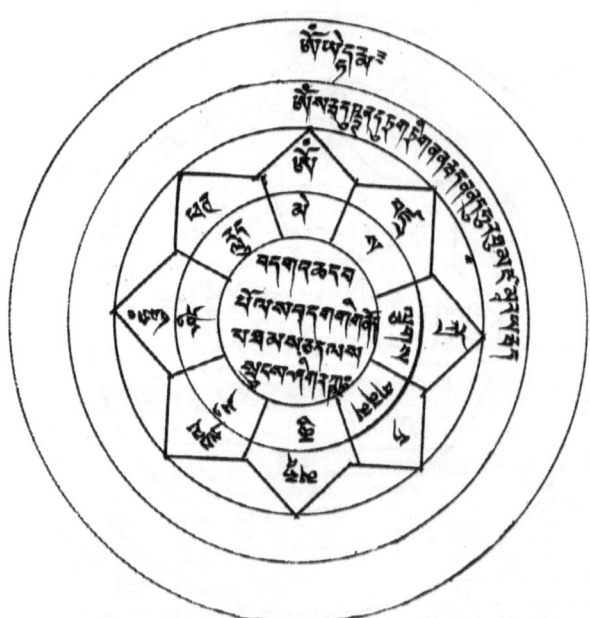

FOUR *CAKRAS* WITH SILK BANNERS

55. The *cakra* which promotes one's effectiveness (*dbang-thang*).

56. The *cakra* which benefits one's body.

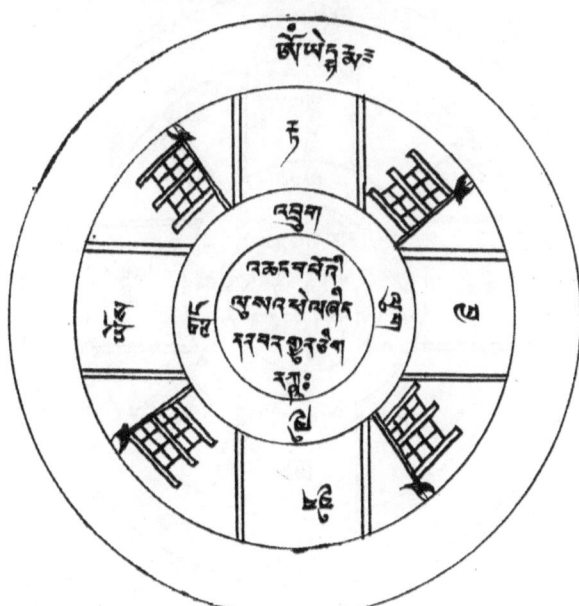

57. The *cakra* which benefits one's life-force (*srog*).

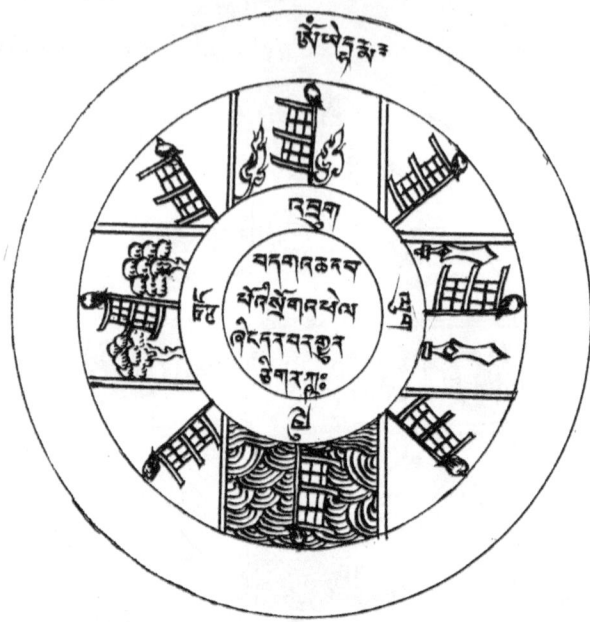

58. The *cakra* which brings good luck (*klung-rta*).

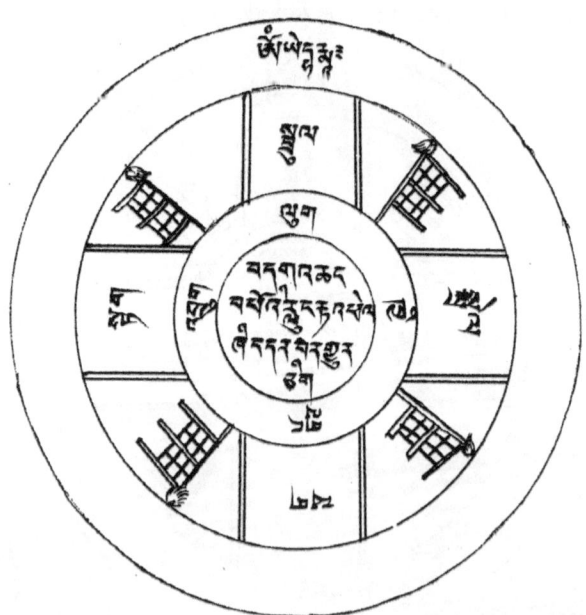

FOUR *CAKRAS* OF FOUR INVOLVEMENTS

59. The *cakra* controlling the eight planets. It is worn while committing a robbery.

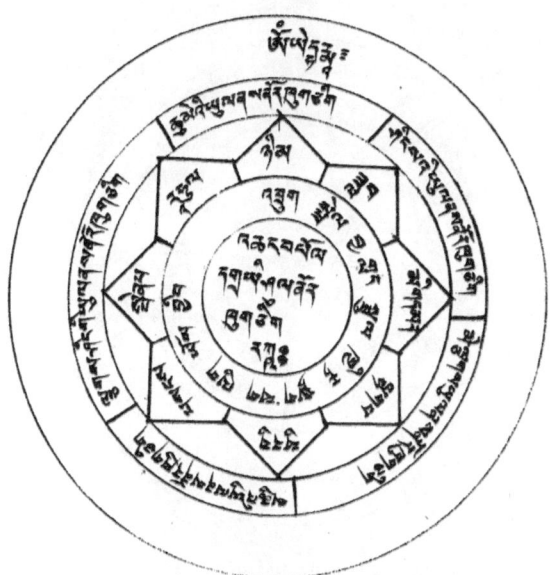

60. The *cakra* which commands the five elements. It is worn when going to battle.

61. The *cakra* harmonizing the lunar mansions (*rgyu-skar*). It is worn when travelling on business.

62. The *cakra* of measures and weights. It is worn when trading goods.

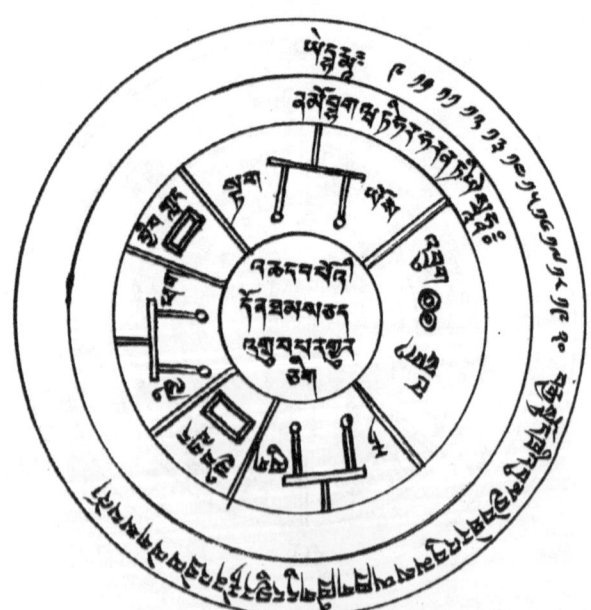

FOUR *CAKRAS* FOR DIFFERENT YOGIC ACTIVITIES

63. The *cakra* with weapons and the fire design. It is worn for protection against evil spirits who disturb meditation.

64. The *cakra* of the four protectors of the portals (*Vajraṅkuśa, Vajrapāśa, Vajrāṃveśa, Vajrasphoṭa*). It is worn during meditation.

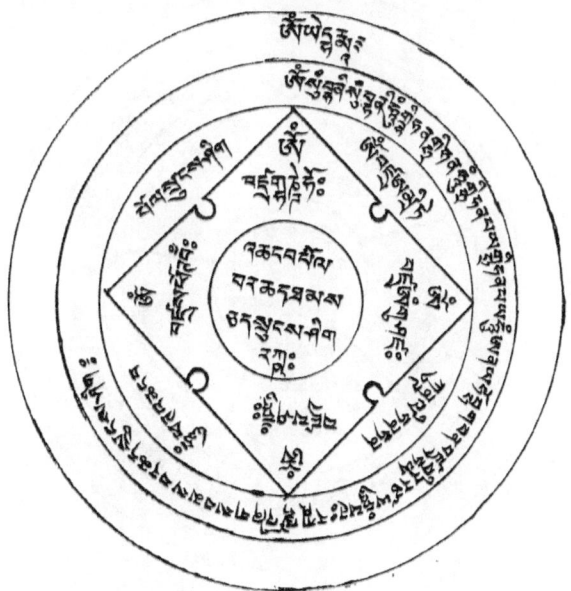

65. The *cakra* of the five goddesses of life (*srid-pa'i lha-mo lnga*). It is worn for protection of the only surviving son. It protects against *chu-sri* who cause harm to children.

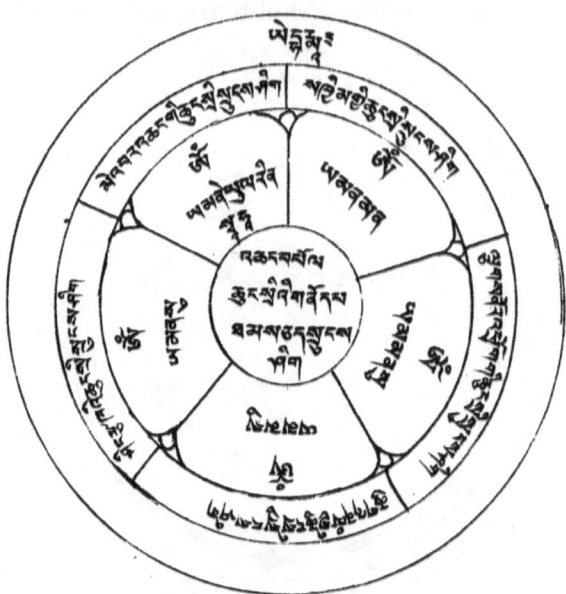

66. The *cakra* of the *Tathāgatas*. It is worn when blessing other people.

TWELVE *CAKRAS* OF THE TWELVE CYCLIC ANIMALS

67. The *cakra* of the monkey. It is worn for protection against epidemics.

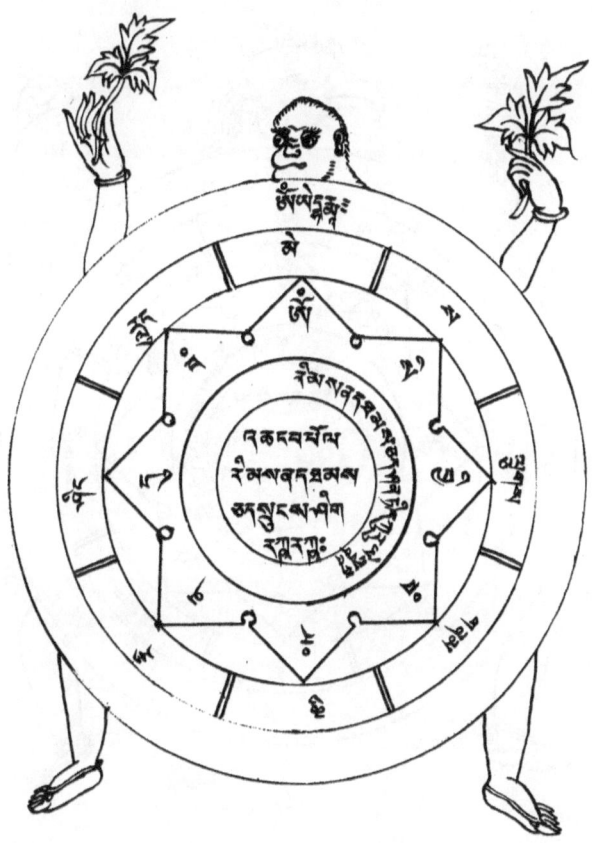

68. The *cakra* of the bird. It is worn for protection against demons (*gdon*).

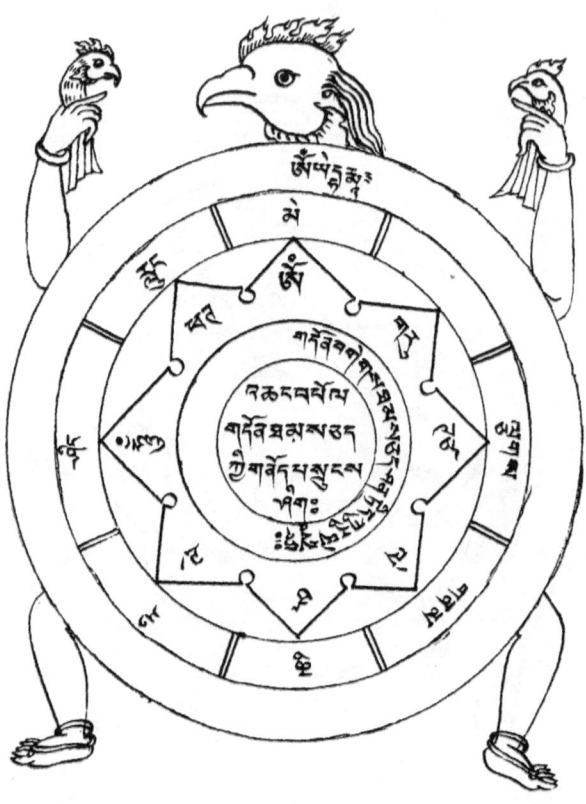

69. The *cakra* of the tiger. It is worn when fearing enemies.

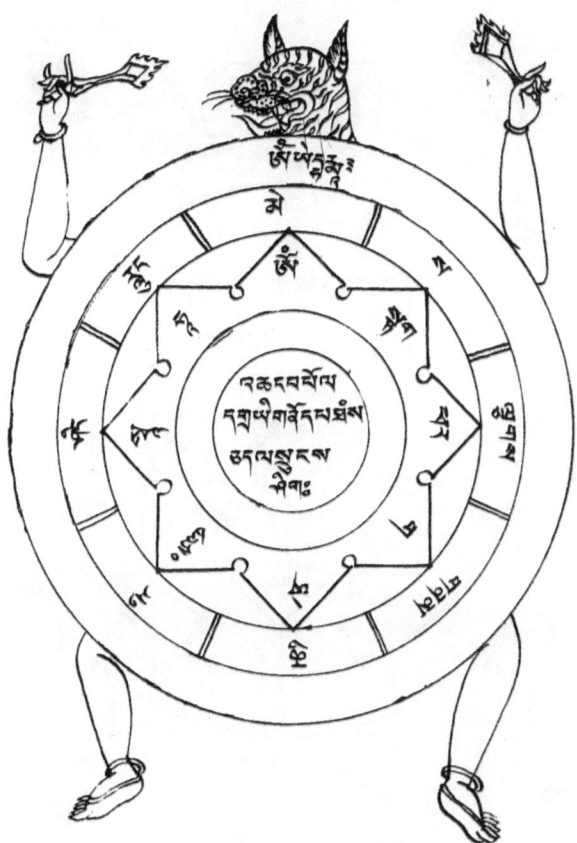

70. The *cakra* of the sheep. It is worn when desiring to increase wealth.

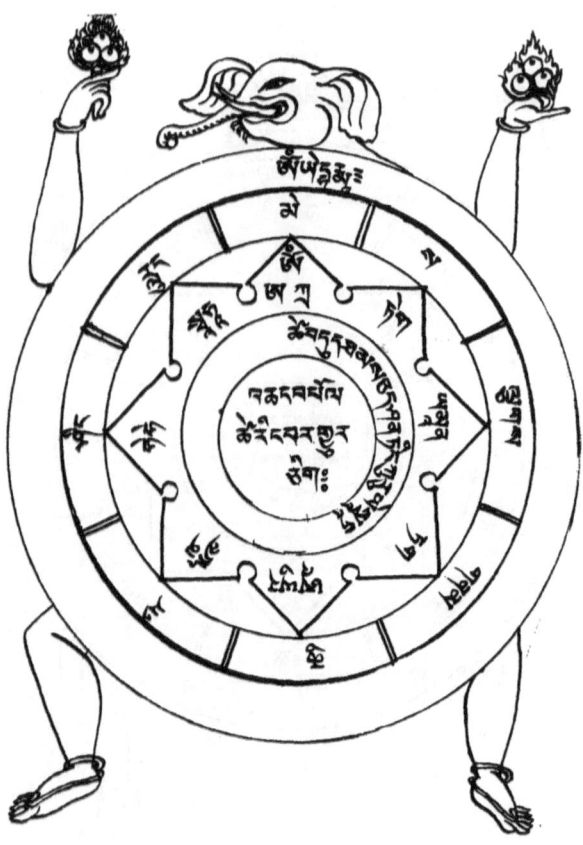

71. The *cakra* of the elephant. It is worn when desiring long life.

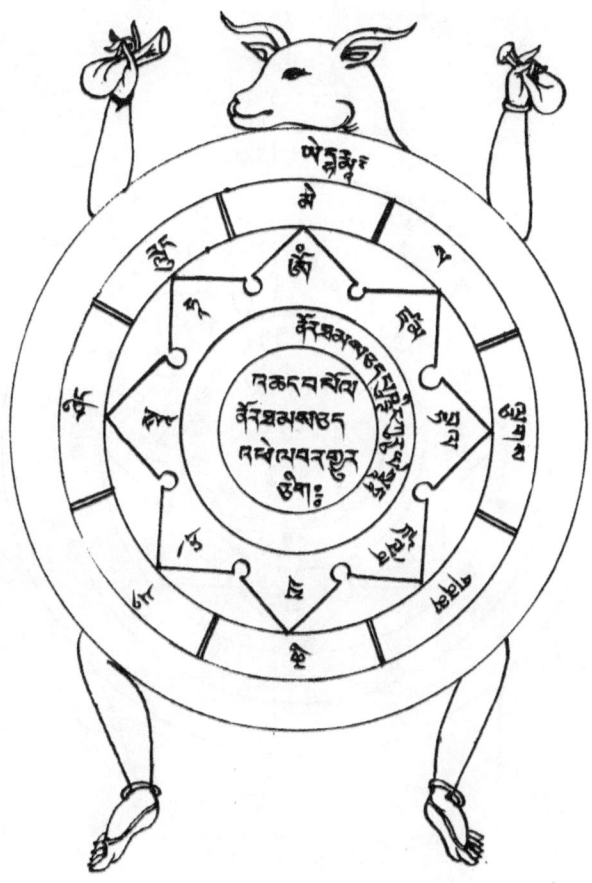

72. The *cakra* of the hare. It is worn when desiring numerous progeny.

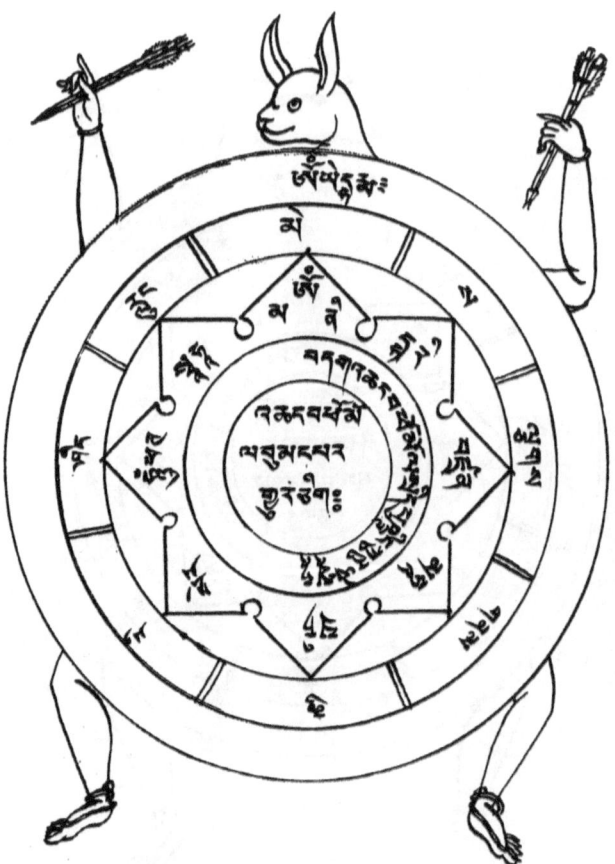

73. The *cakra* of the dragon. It is worn when desiring to possess other people's wealth.

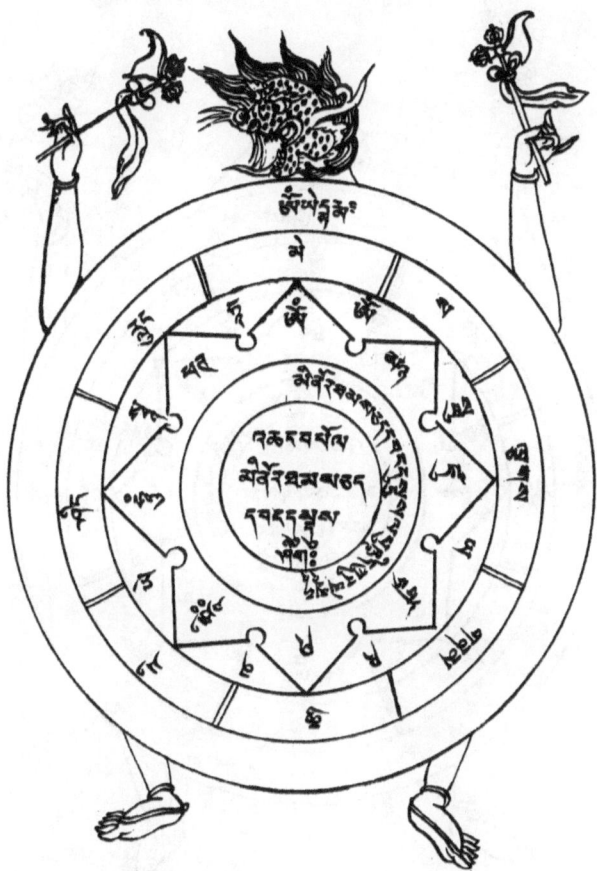

74. The *cakra* of the rat. It is worn for gaining control over people, wealth and victuals.

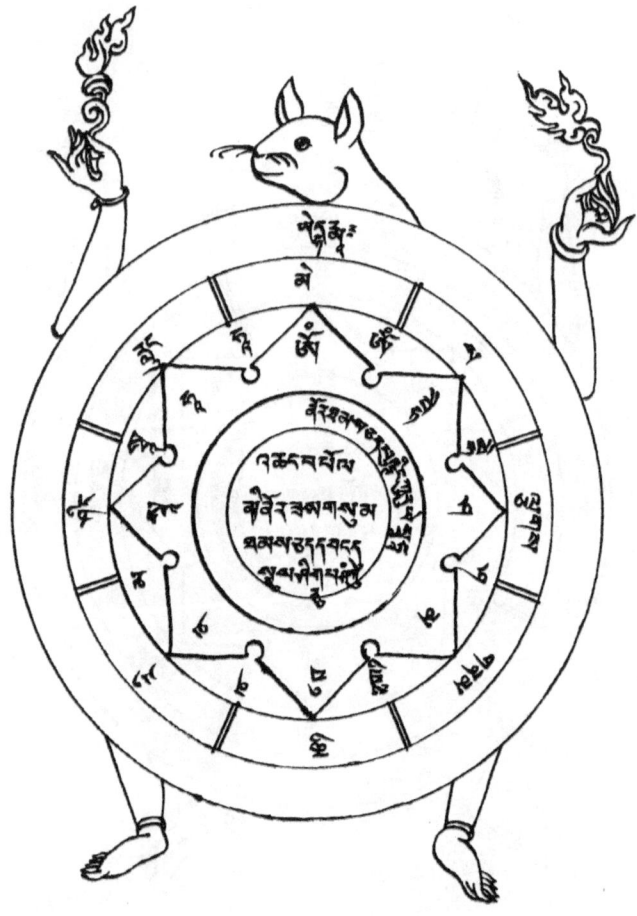

75. The *cakra* of the horse. It is worn for subduing gods and *'dre*.

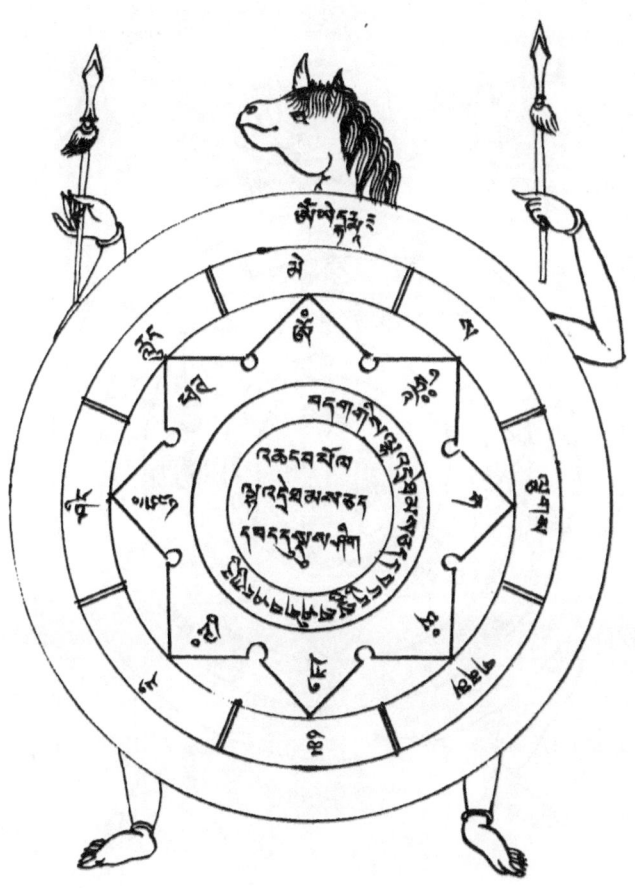

76. The *cakra* of the dog. It is worn when practicing black magic.

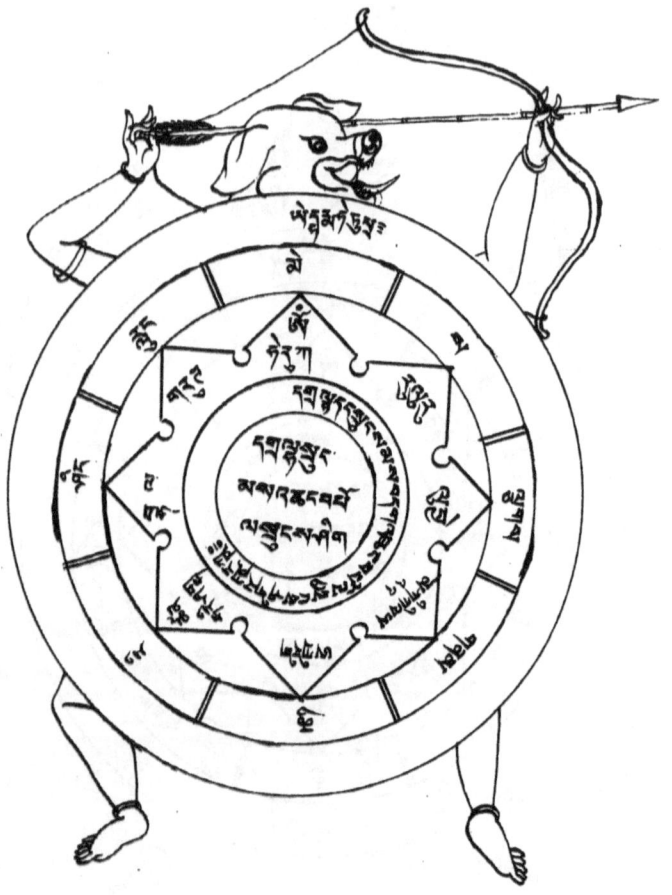

77. The *cakra* of the serpent. It is worn for protection against snake-deities.

78. The *cakra* of the pig. It is worn for protection against lightning and hail-storms.

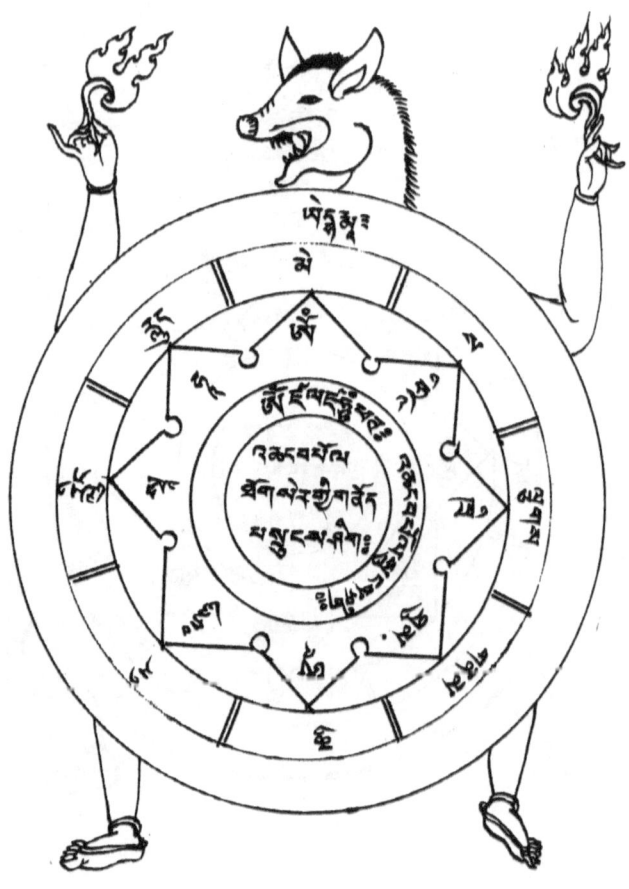

FOUR *CAKRAS* WHICH COUNTERACT EVIL

79. The *cakra* of the 'four fighters' and the syllable *Phaṭ*. It is worn when travelling to evil destinations.

80. The *cakra* of the 'four fighters' and the four elements. It is worn when taking perjurious oaths.

81. The *cakra* of the four goddesses and the *phur-pa*. It is worn for averting imprecations and magical activities.

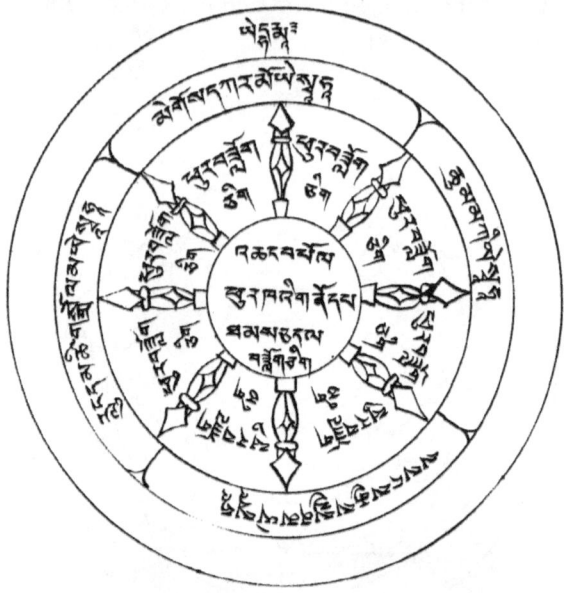

82. The *cakra* with a crossed *vajra* and the syllable *Bhyo*. It is worn for averting maledictions.

FOUR *CAKRAS* WHICH PREVENT DAMAGES.

83. The *cakra* with the calendar chart laid out. It is worn when wishing to benefit all people.

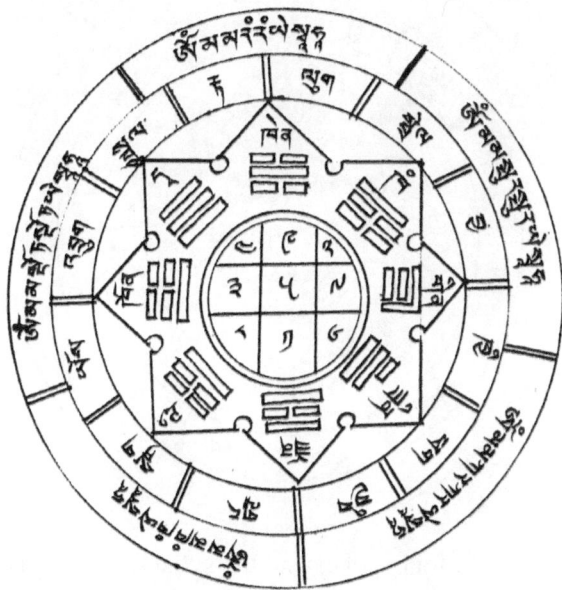

84. The *cakra* with eight spokes and the syllable *Bruṃ*. It is worn when working in the fields.

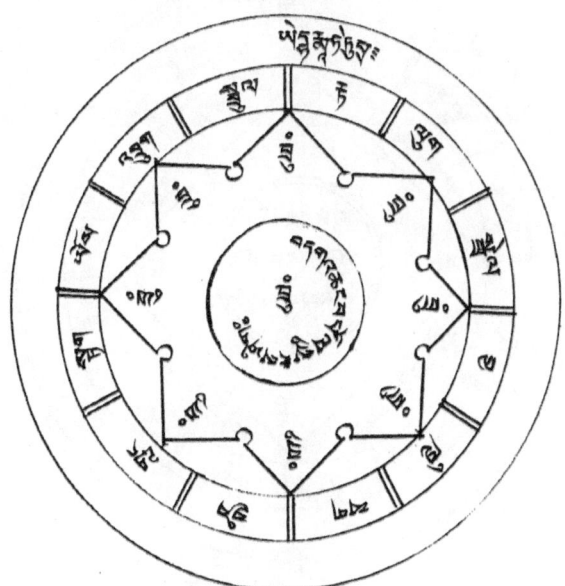

85. The *cakra* with a crossed *vajra* and the syllable *Raṃ*. It is worn when ploughing fields.

86. The *cakra* with four spokes and the syllable *Raṃ*. It is worn for protection against the harm caused by *sa-bdag*, *klu* and *gnyan*.

FOUR *CAKRAS* WHICH PROTECT AGAINST THE DECLINE OF ONE'S LIFEFORCE, BODY, EFFECTIVENESS AND GOOD LUCK

87. The *cakra* of long life and the syllable *Bhruṃ*. It is worn when one's life-force is declining.

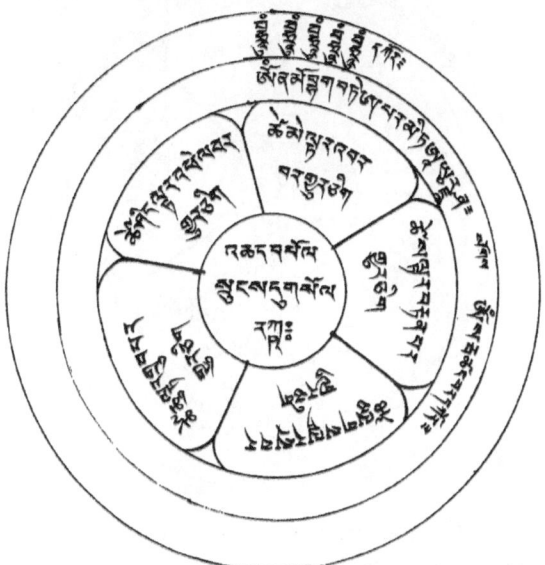

88. The *cakra* of Goddess *Parṇaśabarī*. It is worn when one's body is decaying.

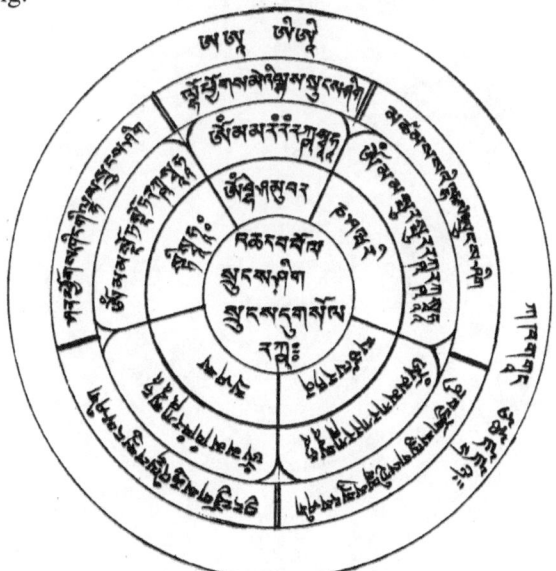

89. The *cakra* of the Five Goddesses. It is worn when one's effectiveness is declining.

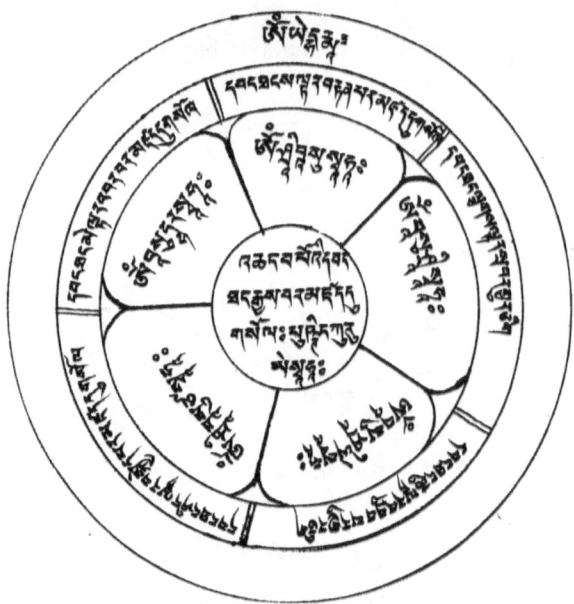

90. The *cakra* of the 'four fighters' and the syllable *Bhyo*. It is worn when one's good luck is declining.

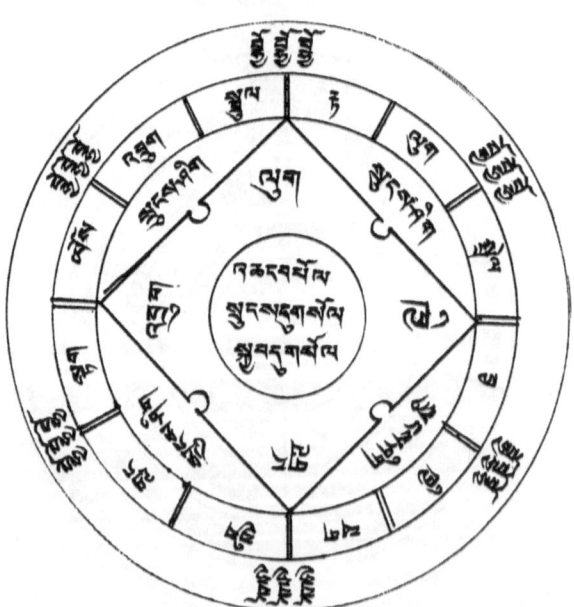

FIVE *CAKRAS* WHICH BIND THE MOUTH (*KHA'-'CHING*)

91. The *cakra* against hail-storms. It is drawn on a peepul tree or a willow. It should face the sky and be smeared with melted butter.

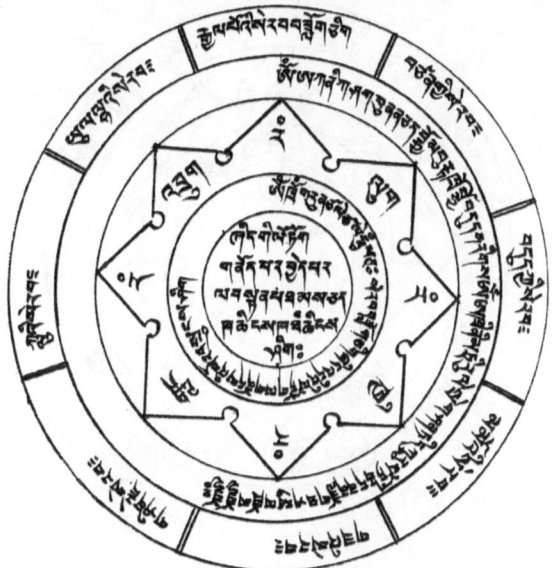

92. The *cakra* against animals which damage crops. After the consecration it should be hidden in a hole in the fields.

93. The *cakra* which binds the mouths of the wolves. It is tied on the necks of horses and cattle afraid of wolves.

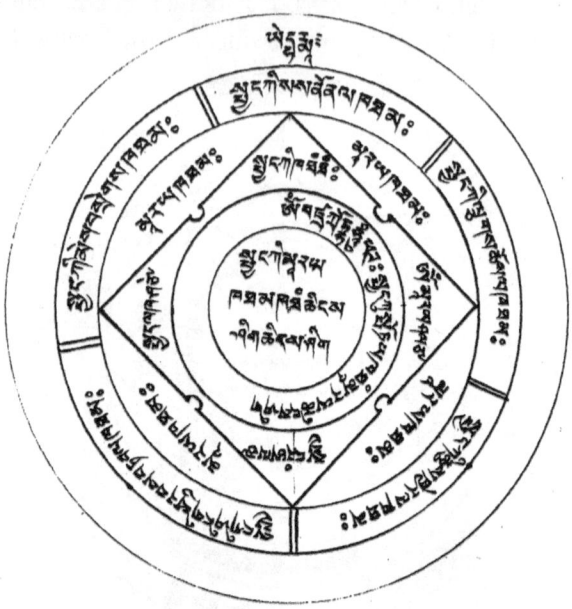

94. The *cakra* for protecting *chang* and curds from turning sour. It is placed under containers of *chang* or curds.

95. The *cakra* for having progeny. It is placed under beds.

CAKRAS OF BODY, SPEECH, MIND, EXCELLENT QUALITIES (*YON-TAN*), AND EFFECTIVE ACTS (*'PHRIN-LAS*)

96. The *cakra* of the body. It should be attached to the crown of the head. It is very powerful and beneficial when staying in evil places.

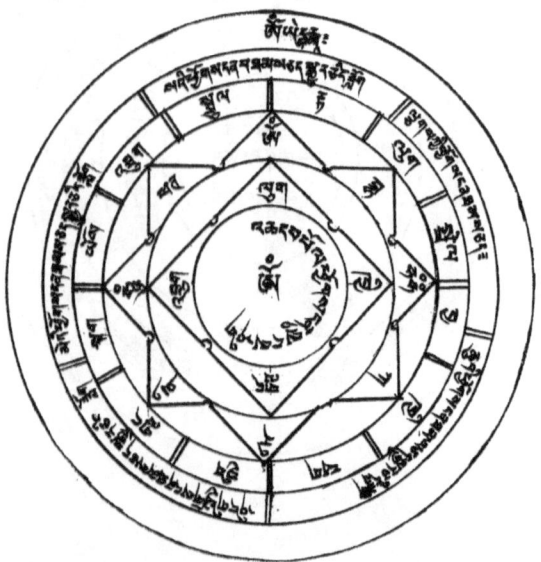

97. The *cakra* of the speech. It is worn around the neck. It destroys evil resulting from taking oaths.

98. The *cakra* of the mind. It is worn on the body. It protects against magical activities and curses.

99. The *cakra* of the body. It protects against evil places.

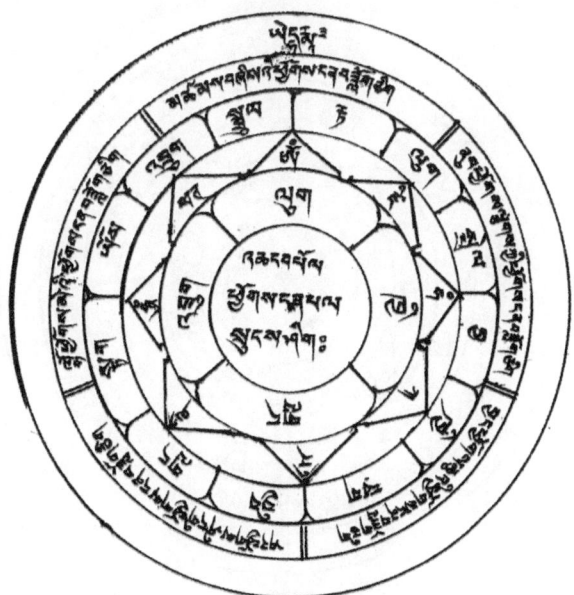

100. The *cakra* of the body. It protects against plagues and epidemics.

101. The *cakra* of the excellent qualities (*yon-tan*). It protects against weapons.

102. The *cakra* of the effective acts (*'phrin-las*). It protects against poisoned weapons in battle.

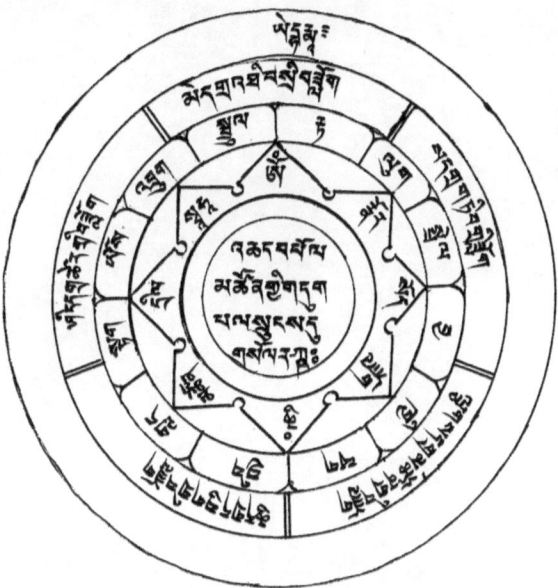

SELECTED GLOSSARY

Abbreviations:

A.- refers to the numbers of the amulets both in the English and in the original Tibetan source texts.

C.- refers to the numbers of the *cakras* in the same way as indicated above.

dkor-'dre – *'dre* which deprive of wealth, C. 46

bskrad-gzir – fierce rites and activities, A. 61

kha-mchu – court case, dispute, C. 39

gi-vang (ghi-vang) – gall stone, A. 29

god-kha – loss (eg. sudden loss of cattle), A. 65

god-'dre – *'dre* who cause losses of different kinds, A. 65

'gab-'dre – *'dre* who follow people. They cause harm to other people and not necessarily to those whom they follow. A. 90

'grul-'dre – *'dre* who accompany people. A. 90; see previous word.

'gron-bu (=mgron-bu) – cowrie; in early times used as money. A. 16

rgan-*sri* – *sri* who cause harm to old people. A 43

rgya-po (ra rgya-po) – spotted goat. A. 12, 42, 47.

rgyal-'gong – a class of spirits; hybrid between rgyal-po and 'gong. A. 27

chu-'dre – *'dre* who live in water. A. 88

chu-shing – drift wood. A.8

nye-'byed – to cause division between relatives and friends. A. 60

gtad – 'evil spells'. Generally it refers to people who make a linga, write down evil spells and wishes, place it in a horn or wrap in a cloth and place it on an enemy's property or under the house. A. 33

lto-'dre – *'dre* who cause hunger and thirst by taking the essence of food. A. 29, 100

thab-mkhon – displeasure of the hearth-god. Offence against the thab-lha (hearth-god) is made by cooking dirty food which overflows onto the fire. People who commit such offences suffer from headaches or sores on their faces. A. 42

dar-sri – *sri* who cause harm ot people who are in the prime of life. A. 45

gdong-'dre – *'dre* who travel ahead of people. A. 90. See 'gab-'dre.

lde-gu (lde-bu) – Sanskrit khanda, candied sugar. A. 29

mnan-pa – evil of oppression; similar to gtad, mthu, and bskrad. A. 59

phur-kha – magic activities. C. 81

pho-shi gri-po – 'ghost' of a man killed with a knife. A. 20

ba-bla – arsenic. A. 65

byad-kha – imprecation. C. 81

brag-ca – echo. C. 97

bon – callus (medical term). A. 35, 41

bya-po mtha'-lu – fine cock. A. 24

bra-ba – rodent. A. 76

bla-brdol – sleep-talking. A. 80

blud-bu – pouch made of animal skin; the hide should be skinned off in one piece without cuts or holes. A. 10

mi-kha – gossip. C. 38

mo-shi gri-mo – 'ghost' of a woman killed with a knife. A. 21

rmongs-tshe – cat. A. 49

smyo-'dre – *'dre* who cause insanity. A. 74

mdze-'dre – *'dre* who cause leprosy. A. 23

zhing-lpags – human skin. A. 60, 62

gzhon-sri – *sri* who cause harm to young people. A. 44

ri'u-tshe – young goat. A. 44

shi-'dre – *'dre* of a dead person. C. 52

shing-kun – extract from garlic. A. 37, 70

gshin-'dre – a dead person who becomes a *'dre*; deceased person's 'spirit' taking possession of a living person. A. 13

gshed-bzhi – 'four fighters'; astrological term referring to the four animals placed to the four corners of the calendar chart; they are sheep, dog, dragon, and ox. C. 5, 10, 79, 80

sad-langs – sleep-walking. A. 80

sri'u – the only surviving son. C. 65

srub-shing – 'rock-shrab'; perhaps same as Sanskrit *sruvāvṛksa* – the tree sruva, A. 14

sre-mo – an animal from the same family as mongoose. A. 10

gson-'dre – *'dre* of living people. A. 18, 19

bse-rag – proper name of lto-'dre. A. 29

ABOUT THE AUTHOR

Tadeusz Skorupski was born in France in 1945. He received his pre-university education in Poland. After completing his university degrees in History of Philosophy and Theology at different universities in Poland, Canada and Italy, he embarked on Oriental Studies in 1972 at the School of Oriental and African Studies, University of London. In 1978, he was awarded a Ph.D. degree in Sanskrit and Tibetan Buddhist Literature. During the period 1978-1982 he was employed as a Research Fellow at the School of Oriental and African Studies, London. The research was sponsored and financed by the Leverhulme Trust. He is an author of numerous articles and books on Tibetan Culture. At the present he pursues further research of Tibetan Buddhism in association with the Institute of Tibetan Studies, Tring, U.K., and sponsored by the British Academy.

www.ingramcontent.com/pod-product-compliance
Lightning Source LLC
Chambersburg PA
CBHW022014160426
43197CB00007B/420